Faith Full

A Memoir of Arletta Clutteur, The White Dove

Lyndsey Clutteur DePalma

 Liveliest Press ● Falls Church, Virginia ● 2020

Faith Full: A Memoir of Arletta Clutteur (The White Dove)

by Lyndsey Clutteur DePalma

Published by

Liveliest Press

6312 Seven Corners Center #144

Falls Church, Virginia 22044

www.livelistpress.com

ISBN: 978-1-7332584-2-5

First printing

MANUFACTURED IN THE UNITED STATES OF AMERICA

To Grandma

Table of Contents

Faith Full

Blessings in the
Spirit of Love

Arletta Clutter
White Dove

Foreword

Song written in 1989 after asking the Lord what she could possibly do when she's too old to bring joy to others. Her thoughts went to wine (that gets better with age as she understood it) and champagne. Other words like "celebration" and "miracle" came and that's when it gelled. She felt excitement because she made the connection to when Jesus turned water into wine at the wedding feast in Canaan. In other words, if you're thirsty, share a message of Jesus, which is what she proudly did.

When a child is born, its first emotions are that of love and trust. It is through life's experience that the child learns hate and fear. My grandmother had more than a small child's share of reasons to abandon her loving heart and grow cold, allowing anger or despair to predominate, but still at age 84 at the time of this published memoir, it is intact, beating strong. The body that she carries, while changed over the years, still pulses the same blood through that steadfast heart and despite her hardships, life's lessons, even criticism for her pursuits. She has not changed. Rebounding from cancer with three babies at home, she has not changed. Running a business without a computer, she has not changed. Learning to pick herself up, find a way to carry out her ambitions, and be the light she believes is being asked of her… her entire life...she has not changed. She hasn't needed to adapt. Never to be deterred, with the faith of a mustard seed and proud ties to her roots, the simplicity of living in the time she grew up, and a heart that beats mainly for the Lord but also her family, her community, *and* the world, she has stayed true to all of these things, especially to herself.

Arletta Mae Whetzel Clutteur, otherwise known as The White Dove, and has been of service to others for as long as, what seems to me as I interviewed her about her life, she was old enough to tie her own shoes. She was the eldest of 8 children and was raised in the mountains of the Shenandoah Valley. She was given this namesake "White Dove" from her late husband Jim, at the early age of 16 because of her orientation around peace and God's love that he recognized in her early on. Being of service comes in many forms and fashions, but most uniformly is the never-missed opportunity to tell a story about the way God speaks to her and His deep love for her.

These pages, while also oriented around bird quotes and her music lyrics, are a tribute to her legacy, and how simple and glorious life can be when everything is done from and for love. Time does march on, but there's a simplicity of time when a rare bird like my grandma is writing the song.

This simplicity is a lost way of life. Lucky for me and those fortunate enough to know her, she is still going strong, baking for charities and following her heart to remind us of how life was and still can be, thanks to the glory of God. We are happiest when we do things of and from love and we find the most purpose when our heart is open for us to receive messages from our Source (in her case, God through Jesus Christ). The truth this book aims to uncover is that in 2020, the world may look and feel different, but through our actions, it can be as texturized and wholesome as it was for our ancestors. Generations ahead may not understand this way of living in a fast paced, tech-driven world; however, we can take note of some exceptional examples of our humanity, and connect those examples back to that simple, love-driven way of life that our ancestors knew before status and superficial achievement became a thing.

It is my goal in this book to first and foremost honor my extraordinary grandmother while she's still on this earth to inspire us. She is the champagne lady after all, and while she wrote that song to honor the feast of God and the best wine that was saved for last, it's also a perfect song to represent her effervescent inspiration. While in her view all things are accomplished through God, for me, I also think they're accomplished through having healthy examples of taking risks, being a hero, and authenticity for a person to believe what's possible. Also in this book, I want to honor the history and the time period she was building her legacy in. To ask her, she says she hasn't done any of the facts that follow to gain recognition. It was always something on her heart. Imagine if we would all stop what we're doing to write a letter to the president of a foreign country or donate our precious sleep to multiple causes a week, because it was on our heart? Imagine how these acts would make us feel, our communities enveloped in this love, and our own legacies for having been inspired to do the best we can. Don't get me wrong, she's able to find energy in corners of her being that are inaccessible by many humans, but her consistent love of all is something to regard. Imagine if recording all these efforts could inspire others to make their time on this planet more meaningful by reflecting on impact in spite of adversity, thanks to staying connected to her divine purpose and compounded with love. Readers of all walks of life can find some music in her stories of being an instrument of God's love. Yet even nonreligious readers can appreciate their own capacity to live joyfully with purpose in their hearts by understanding that of Arletta Clutteur's.

Arletta and Lyndsey before church, Photo Credit Unknown

Part I

My Heart is a Throne

My heart is a throne, he lives in my home
I'm not ashamed me in, can't you see
He took me in, forgave my sins
Forgave a sinner like me.
Wherever I go, seeds of love I sow
And you just wait and see
Someday we'll grow that others will know
Who's speaking to me.

I don't need a book, I don't have to look
To see what words to say
For can't you see, he speaks to me,
In a very special way.

Now if you let him come in (and he is your true friend)
Many will turn away
Don't follow them, they're not your true friend
But let us pray, when that day comes,
They will have a light on their throne!

My heart is a throne, he lives in my home
I'm not ashamed me in, can't you see
He took me in, forgave my sins
Forgave a sinner like me.
Wherever I go, seeds of love I sow
And you just wait and see
Someday we'll grow that others will know
Who's speaking to me.

© 1979 Arletta M Clutteur
Written in 1979 when she realized God was speaking through her.

Chapter 1: Finding Flight

Early identity

"Before I can live with other folks I've got to live with myself. The one thing that doesn't abide by majority rule is a person's conscience."

- Harper Lee, <u>To Kill a Mockingbird</u>

Even though there wasn't much going on in the hills of Virginia's Shenandoah Valley in 1936 when Arletta Mae Whetzel was born, there was history being made. The surname Whetzel existed in the valley for generations. The nearest town was Dovesville (later renamed Bergton) and was proximal to Cootes Store, a rendezvous point for working men given its location (a mile) from Brocks Gap. Historically, the area she was born to was populated with farmers in the nearby town Brocks Gap has the Shenandoah River (transport system for merchants) to thank for its popularity. The floods of her birth year took out many of the barns and cottages in that area, but thankfully the elevation of the mountains allowed this story to take shape and become a springboard for a story of many facets, all centering around a common current.

When she was a small child, she would play near the creek that ran near her home, making mud pies and dreaming she was making a big meal for a lot of people. She would use her grandma and granddaddy's snuff glasses to fill with water to set the table. She would say "Dear God, let everyone come to this table to eat." Today, she can see where her spirit was leading her, but didn't understand this at the time. This may have been from her own hunger or it could be that she was deeply connected to her life's work.

Early Morn

A new day was born ~

April's gentle winds blow tender leaves,
The birds sing a melody as they rest in the trees

~ I felt the freshness of the breeze

Beauty of Nature everywhere~
Fragrance of flowers was like perfume
Refreshing as the fallen dew

The Sun gave light and warmth~
A Gift from God for all to see,
A Garden of Beauty for you and me.

Arletta Clutteur, April 2014
*15326

Arletta's defining moments are plentiful. She'd say that the examples of this entire book are monumental, pivotal, and meaningful. Not in a prideful way, but in an everything-is-connected, with purpose, and punctuated by signs from the Lord all around her. She's religious by fate but patriotic by choice. When asked how she grew to become so patriotic (long before two of her sons served in the armed forces, and despite that her husband had served), her response was that the love for her country was born right alongside her love for her community, and her love for her Creator. "You can't have one without the rest" is her simple answer to indicate that defending a country is defending a community, and believing in a higher power is what makes sometimes difficulty and sacrifice worth it. Indeed, a simple answer to a very complex observation of life and vastness. And to be here, in this vastness, we have to know what's important and what our roles are.

Are We Proud?

Are we proud to be here today?

FAITH FULL

Are we proud of the jobs we do?
Are we proud of the people that work side by side,
That work with me and you?

Are we proud when we scheme and do things of deceit?
Are we proud of the secrets we keep?
Are we proud of the way we treat others today,
Are we proud of the words we say?

Are we proud to be seen with the sick and the poor?
Are we proud to share comfort and food from our store?
Are we proud of all the thing we have in our home,
Or are we too proud to let our light shine?

Are we proud of Jesus who carried the cross
For sinners like us, that our souls won't be lost?

Now what if Jesus would stop by today?
Would we welcome Him in or send Him away?
Would be a guest at our table to eat,
Or would we send him away like a tramp on the street?

Would we ask him to join in a game of cards,
Or ask him to have a drink at the bar?

Or would we say "Can't you see!
I have no time, I am tired and want to watch TV."
Or would we say, "Jesus, I am proud that you have come,
I want to welcome you into my home,"

In the Spirit of Love,
A Friend

©1979 /s/ White Dove

She views her patriotism and community-centric mindset as a natural biproduct of just looking around. She celebrates all that she sees, and it comes as no surprise that she notices more things because she's looking around with happy eyes. Seeing the face of Jesus in the clouds, a cross in the trees or a heart-shaped stone. We find what we search for, and what we focus on gets stronger. One way her identity was solidified was through her focus on seeing things in a beautiful light. I remember as a young girl spending time in her cellar workshop where she would make beautiful moss/nature covered creations (often wishing wells) which she referred to as her "woodland creations." She would collect animal figurines, organic or natural elements and build something more beautiful. She would title the creations things like "Wandering" and "Resting" and "Searching." In an article from the Daily News Record on October 16, 1973 she was quoted "I just don't understand how I came to make these things or why they mean so much to me." But like her poetry, her woodland art, as inspired by that first heard shaped stone with the mushroom, was one of her "gifts." The same article quotes her saying "I just want my work to be a labor of love, just as developing Bennett's Run with friends and neighbors was." Bennett's Run is where the original woodland creation was encased and displayed to remind visitors of the harmony the hollow represented. When I asked her why all this 'stuff' in her woodland workshop she explained that in the early 70s, her birthday wish was that every heart could be filled with love and joy…that there could be unity and peace among all nations. She then asked her husband for a real wishing well for her birthday. The original wishing well (built at Bennett's Run, VA by family, neighbors and friends in 1972) was featured in the Daily News Record in 1972. A year later, in 1973 she would begin making the woodland creations in earnest, sending miniature wishing wells to the White House as a gift to President Jimmy Carter, to Secretary-General Kurt Waldheim in the United Nations, and later tot President Ronald Reagan. My mom even delivered a wishing well to the Virginia governor Chuck Robb in 1985. In the process of creating these wells, she would carefully select, wash and dry and place each rock on the wishing wells, blessing each creation with a prayer.

Mrs. Arletta Clutteur holds one of her favorite woodland creations, entitled "Searching."

Arletta's picture in the Daily News Record Article featuring her woodland creations.

In asking why she went so far out of her way to ship these 10x12 inch wells (imagine the cost), she remarked that even the leaders need a little hope in their lives. The question I should have asked was how does she find time to do all these things, while raising children, working often several jobs, and supporting her family or church community? Later in life, after she'd had time to reflect, her answer was that it doesn't feel like work when you're collecting the beauty around you to make more beauty. She didn't know why she was so drawn to beauty, but after writing this book for her now, and learning more about her childhood and the person behind all the action she does, another motivation to do these seems to strengthen her connection to her mother earth. In doing so, here was another way to be proud, just like of her community and country, and therefore continuously invite those beautiful, appreciative messages from her Creator.

Love
Love is a bridge over which we pass
In happier lands
Love is a mountain from which we reach
God's ever-waiting hands.
Love is a valley fertile and green
Where life's best things can grow.

Love is a harbor safe and serene
(for loving hearts to know)
Love is a song that lifts the heart
Above life's daily cares
Love is a power, sacred and real
That blesses like a prayer.

God is love.

© *Arletta Clutteur*

And whenever our heart is touched, it softens. Arletta walked around with a soft heart, finding beauty, and that cycle perpetuated on itself. When we feel so moved, we feel a part of something larger, and that further solidifies our belonging.

Did Arletta's mother, raising a daughter without the help of her estranged husband, teach her to view this way? Quite likely. But as I stand back from her stacks and stacks of accolades and articles of her positive doings and reflections, I have a hunch she may have been born this way. Born to Elva Whetzel in the hills of Bergton, VA, with the nearest stoplight more than 30 miles away and the general store more than 7 miles away, Arletta and her mother had very little to their name. Her mother tended to chicken houses and sold milk can redemptions to make ends meet. Later when she married Arletta's stepfather Charlie, he helped support their family by cutting pulp wood after being discharged from the military. He also did odds and ends and drove his old truck for Rockingham Poultry and made apple butter for the general store. Arletta was the eldest of 9: she had six younger brothers and two younger sisters. In order of birth, Charlie Jr (deceased), Garnet, Lonnie, Bobbie, Ivan (deceased), Allen (deceased), Geneta and Eula. A neat story about Eula, is that she is the same age as Arletta's youngest son David and her second oldest sister, Geneta, is the same age as Charlie, Arletta's second oldest son.

While Arletta wouldn't know her father's side of the family until decades later when her Aunt Hazel looked her up and found her after watching a commercial Arletta was in for then employer, Wal-Mart. Arletta was working as a greeter one day when a lady approached her. The lady said, "you're Arletta." My grandmother replied, "yes, but who are you?" From then on, Arletta enjoyed going on bus tours with her aunt and daughters, and they became cousins late in life, as if they had always known each other. Still, her half-siblings were her life and to this day, through upholding holiday traditions, family reunions and general support, consider each other close-knit. It's a delight to get them in a room and start the laugh engine. This group of brothers and sisters love to laugh and find humor in just about anything. When taking pictures for this memoir, she told the photographer (Brandy Somers Photography), "They called me a nut years ago, and I'm so glad, because [that means] I can be cracked..." This sukha, which is sanskrit for happiness for no reason, is something that she carries with her, even when not in the company of her equally joyful, playful and equally silly family members.

VOL. 167 NO. 8   New Market, Va.   *1973 February 21.*   Wednesday, Evening

MR. AND MRS. JAMES CLUTTEUR rest in Bennett's Run Friendly Grove Picnic Area. The area, that now includes a wishing well and shelter, began with Mrs. Clutteur's idea to hold a reunion of all the Bennett's Run residents and relatives.

Arletta and her husband Jim in the hills of Bennett's Run, with the wishing well in the background (image of the newspaper article published February 21, 1973.

Arletta classifies her upbringing village as "mountain neighbors" who looked out for each other and would harvest together. They lived off of the land as much as possible and loaded up the neighbor's horse and went down to the "old store" to trade their bounty. They never sold it, but for fun, they would make taffy for hours and hours. She recalls her stepfather Charlie selling big baskets of green beans to help pay for medical bills. As a family activity, they tended to their garden, with grandparents to grandchildren all working to keep it beautiful. This way of life remained. The family house remained in the family and as I recalled lifetimes later, playing in the same barn that housed the pigs that were turned to sausage in the kitchen a few hundred feet away. Even though they made most food and clothing, Grandma recalls a story of her mother not being able to afford anything for Christmas, but she managed to acquire a doll and two pieces of candy both wrapped under the tree. That Christmas was a pivotal part of her origin story as we'll see later in her motivations. For her childhood, Arletta was content with the things they had. She didn't need a lot because in her words, she "didn't know what a lot was."

While toys of the era were the new slinky or tinkertoys, Arletta was not aware of such entertainment because instead of playing with other kids, she was often caring for her younger siblings or eventually in formal babysitting jobs. When asked if she had a best friend growing up, she said of course it was her mom, but beyond that the only person she could think of was her teacher at Bennett's Run School, Irene Halterman. She was kind, was always there to listen to the children and was an understanding mentor to the kids of the mountains. The neighbor's children were around and Arletta did play with them often, but with her stepdad away at the war (World War II), much of her playtime was expended. This also didn't faze Arletta because being of service was in her DNA. Siblings, even twins, are studied to have been born with a certain character and behavioral tendencies. With the exact same upbringing and influence, two children can take on very different preferences, motivations and ideals. Our world is lucky that Arletta was born wanting to be helpful and impactful (although this later trait is one that she is still too humble to fully accept). While her siblings were also helpful, Arletta assumed a lot of responsibility and did so, lovingly. Her memories of her childhood are fond – she recalls singing and praying together before bed, even while her sibling's dad, Arletta's stepfather, was away serving in the military.

Arletta was quoted in a newspaper article much later in life as having had a dream to hold gatherings and be a peacemaker even as a little girl. She knew what her gifts were, even with no money and no real exposure to others who could inspire her ambitions. Her contact with the 'outside' world was from her family's battery radio, where she recalls mostly hearing about blackouts during the war, and certainly not of poor farmgirls rising up beyond their means to give so much to others.

Her luck and her story changed at the age of 16, when she was celebrating New Year's Eve at the movie house in Broadway, Virginia. There, she met the blue-eyed, handsome soldier James Clutteur Sr, discharged from the Army where he had served at Fort Sill, Oklahoma and in Germany. Their chance encounter involved her saying hello very warmly because she thought she knew this handsome man. It turns out she mistook him for someone else, but he used that greeting as a chance to become friends. He followed her into the movie and ended up driving her home that frigid night. She originally protested (as any proper lady of this time would do) but thank goodness she acquiesced because that ice-ridden car ride strengthened their bond and they made a point to see each other again the next day. It was love at first sight and they went for drives while they courted in the coming weeks. When she told her mother she thought he was the man she was to marry, her mother asked Jim to take her for a ride. Arletta never knew what was said on that drive, but Elva consented. Arletta saw in Jim kindness and the kind of goodness that someone who embodies those qualities recognizes. As for Jim, he said he knew in a month's time he loved this woman as reported in an article in The Northfork Journal on February 10, 1993 (coverage of their 40th Anniversary). They decided to get married a few weeks later on Valentine's Day, because a big storm was predicted by the Farmer's Almanac for the originally chosen wedding weekend. In her grandfather's words, "a big ole storm is coming so you better get married this weekend instead." As the product of their love and marriage, I find it completely fitting that the Universe and weather system conspired to help them settle on February 14, 1953 to get married. On their wedding day they had less than $5 between them, so did no honeymoon trip and this was for the good because my grandfather needed to return to work as a Shen-Valley Meat Packers truck driver. As newlyweds, they didn't have money to go out, but Arletta recalls that on their anniversary, they would always try to go 'out' somewhere. Even if it was on a drive around town, harkening back to their courtship, they would do something to celebrate the day. Forty years later at their anniversary celebration, the couple dedicated the event to the people who loved them and who helped perpetuate and refuel their love. The couple couldn't partake in their 30th celebration because Jim had broken his back and couldn't attend the party their children had planned for them. So, for their 40th, their friends Kenny and Shirly Emerson orchestrated everything and turned the Broadway Community Center into a veritable chapel. "Jim Honey" had said to her, "if she was nice, he might ask her to marry him again" at the event. She was apparently nice because they renewed their vows 40 years into their marriage.

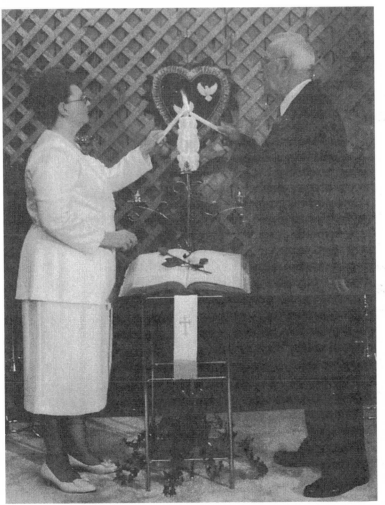

The couple renewing their vows while lighting a unity candle on their 40th anniversary.

Photo credit unknown.

Everyone in attendance received a poem rolled up like a scroll with a mauve ribbon around. Within, the poem included a heartfelt thanks to those who helped foster their love and commemorate their special day.

Ten months and two weeks after their wedding date they welcomed the their first born, Jim Jr. They lived in an apartment for six months on Collicello Street in Harrisonburg, Virginia and then moved into the Mayland/Broadway, Virginia home that she still resides in today. "Cherokee Jim" (his CB Radio handle, and what was painted on his bug guard across is 1990 Ram truck) was exactly the man she predicted he would be when she first met him: a man with a "strong love in his heart and concern for other people," which together, they leveraged their natural inclinations to make a beautiful life full of sharing and caring.

Their life together wasn't extravagant. She recalls in their early days they would fix a big thermos of hot cocoa for sleigh rides and make cookies for the neighborhood children who would come to their house for years to come. For their first Christmas, their small tree had two small packages - a bottle of Old Spice for him and a hairbrush for her. Best of all was the arrival of their newborn baby on December 16th of that first year. She regards the simple things like these as the most vivid of her memories. While simple, they are meaningful, uncomplicated, and what unite us as humans. Decades later when smartphones define our distracted and isolated era, Arletta's coming upness was a time when people really showed up for their neighbor because complex schedules or overachieving goals didn't compete with time invested in your neighbor. A good era indeed, and Arletta feels so lucky to the path she has found herself on. They renewed their vows 40 years later at the Broadway Community Center.

As an editorial note, many folks from the Shenandoah Valley pronounce the family name as "Clutters." I had a chance to clarify and she said that it was pronounced "Clutter" for a period of time, however when Jim was in the service overseas, he had a sergeant who set him straight on the French pronunciation, clu-too-ehr since the U was not at all silent and not as sharp. There was never an S to speak of despite long-timers insisting as much even to this day.

Arletta's purpose for being of service didn't stop when she ended school early to care for her family, or when she met my grandfather and quickly married. It didn't end when she had children back to back (her second son Charles was born 22 months later, and the third born three years after), nor when she and Jim faced illness, respectively. One day early in their marriage, she had a vision to "put seed corn in the bags." They didn't have a lot of money together but shared the vision with Jim because "there is going to be a lot of hungry people someday, and we have to share." He asked no questions and trusted her vision completely, getting to work on the baggies. She saw two tables in this vision and organized a potluck promptly, as she's been moved to do many times since. She makes ham pot pie or cakes and shares with others freely in between organizing benefits for others. Today, when asked about that vision, she believes it was to foretell the homelessness crisis in the nation and some of the benefits of people all around.

Even without a lot of money, her experiences were still rich. She stayed close to the person she was and let that little girl lead her through many acts of service and kindness, even when she didn't have much to give herself. As someone related to someone so generous, I look at this example and believe that you don't have to be born with a silver spoon, you just need to be true to the character you come out as. People tend to evolve a few times through life. If you know Arletta today and are reading this, you can picture the energized, self-starter and faith-driven little girl she always was. Even though some people change in their lifetimes, Arletta has not and in her case, staying the same heart-led girl has made her level of impact consistent over all the decades.

Arletta carrying an advent wreath she made annually for her church community **Photo credit unknown.**

Chapter 2: Motivation

"A bird never flew on one wing." - Proverb

In the early '70s, she was walking in the mountains with her brother Ivan. He was helping her gather materials for her woodland creations when she heard a loud "Arletta" right over her shoulder. She shouted to her brother "What, Ivan" and he from a distance responded he didn't say anything. She knew immediately it was an angel or something sent to get her attention. She stopped in her tracks and said out loud, "Lord use me as you like." Within a few steps she saw a heart shaped rock with a mushroom growing out of the side. To her, and through the lens of finding signs everywhere if you just open your eye and heart, she saw the mushroom as the life He shares with us. She knew she was gifted by the spirit, and that has been one of the key sources of motivation for her acts, but she didn't have the words to describe this "heart of stone". She prayed 'give me the words to say,' and by September of that year, the words poured right out of her. It was well timed because that is when a reporter got word of the heart of stone and wrote an article on the fall of 1973 in the Daily News Record.

Being connected to your purpose and maker is a powerful thing. One doesn't really ask questions, they just do. And do is what Arletta did. She saw turmoil on the local WHSV-TV3 News station and did something about it. She would send prayers to heads of states, make up poems to underscore her prayers of love for the country and their leadership, and go out of her way to raise the vibration of love. She sent a flag she made to President Jimmy Carter, praying for peace during his presidency. It was to symbolize hope. Peace, love and unity – that love sees no distinction in race, color or creed. The flag was then placed in the Jimmy Carter Presidential Library and Museum.

12 DAILY NEWS-RECORD, HARRISONBURG, VIRGINIA
THURSDAY, JUNE 14, 1979

For The President

Arletta M. Clutteur of Rt. 1, Broadway displays a flag identical to one she has sent President Carter for Fathers Day. Mrs. Clutteur designed the flag to symbolize peace and love among nation. It has a red heart and white stars and dove on a dark blue background. One star has a purple center, representing the King of Kings, Mrs. Clutteur said. The seven stars represent the seven churches mentioned in the book of Revelation. Mrs. Clutteur also has released an album of poems and songs.

Given As A Gift - to our Nation

A Fold in the page at the word Flag

News-Record Photo

Article in the Daily News Record, Father's Day, 1979

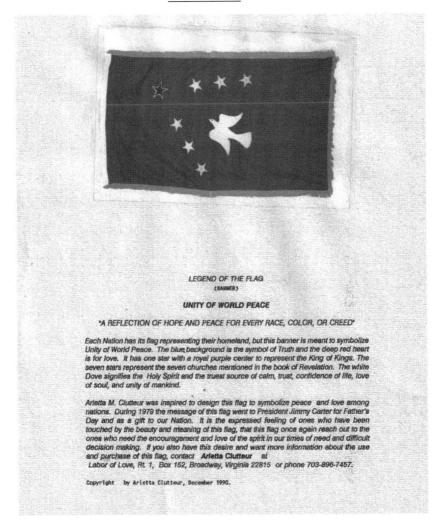

LEGEND OF THE FLAG
(BANNER)

UNITY OF WORLD PEACE

"A REFLECTION OF HOPE AND PEACE FOR EVERY RACE, COLOR, OR CREED"

Each Nation has its flag representing their homeland, but this banner is meant to symbolize Unity of World Peace. The blue background is the symbol of Truth and the deep red heart is for love. It has one star with a royal purple center to represent the King of Kings. The seven stars represent the seven churches mentioned in the book of Revelation. The white Dove signifies the Holy Spirit and the truest source of calm, trust, confidence of life, love of soul, and unity of mankind.

Arletta M. Clutteur was inspired to design this flag to symbolize peace and love among nations. During 1979 the message of this flag went to President Jimmy Carter for Father's Day and as a gift to our Nation. It is the expressed feeling of ones who have been touched by the beauty and meaning of this flag, that this flag once again reach out to the ones who need the encouragement and love of the spirit in our times of need and difficult decision making. If you also have this desire and want more information about the use and purchase of this flag, contact **Arletta Clutteur** *at Labor of Love, Rt. 1, Box 152, Broadway, Virginia 22815 or phone 703-896-7457.*

Copyright by Arletta Clutteur, December 1990.

The flag sent to President Jimmy Carter

For every prayer or gift she would send, she often received a thank you from the recipient, for which she's kept the originals in her safety deposit box. She's offered several of these letters for purpose of this book, found in the appendix. Additional correspondence can be found in the appendix. When interviewing her for this book, she pulled out a binder of copies, pointing out correspondence as recent as 2020 from then President Donald Trump. She exclaimed that she's received all kinds of messages back from Barack (Obama, former President) and proceeded to share several other messages over the 80s, 90s and 2000's. Her efforts and motivation to serve her Lord have not ceased through the decades.

Love is another source of her motivation. Without hesitation, if there was an opportunity to share love through a meal or her songs, she did it with a full and open heart. Imagine if anytime you had a notion or an urge, you followed through, completely. And imagine any place you looked, you were inspired by the beauty or the delight of God's creation. The truth is, we all have that, but most of us have placed our focus on other things. Brain science tells us though that what you focus on gets stronger. And if you focus on work, or success, or any of the number of distractions we allow ourselves in this life, this is what your brain will continue to notice. In other words, we see more of the same. But if you are Arletta and can find something fantastic, even the face of Jesus in cake batter, then surely you will deepen those grooves, and see more of this abundance. She recalls a time when she was planning a reunion and happened to have an enormous sunflower growing in her yard. She cut it down, decorated it, added some elements to make a face, and displayed it prominently at the head of the buffet table at the event. When asked about this interesting table piece, she said "we have everything we need to see beauty and what the sun creates, we just need to see to put it together."

Beauty

If teardrops were roses
Heartaches would be rainbows
The world would be so bright that it would glow.

In the midst of all the glory
A lamb you could see
The Lamb of God, the Light of the World,
No darkness would there be.

The tree of life - the leaves could be medicine
To heal the nations near and far
The lily of the valley the beauty all could share

The living water - flow freely to all that thirsts may drink
The bread of life is given to all that comes to eat.

Oh the people would rejoice
Kneel in prayer
And ask God to save our people
And heal the land here and there

In Peace and Love

Arletta Clutteur, White Dove 15326 5/17/83

When interviewing Arletta for this book, a lot of standard questions to get elderly talking (like what was your fondest memory), were not what you'd expect. She didn't take a lot of vacations in her life (before White Dove Tours) so her responses were highlights around how her bed broke on her first night as a married couple with Jim Sr. [Sidebar: The next day the neighbors asked what on earth they were doing the night before: she didn't realize he had not fully assembled the bed in the event she wanted it positioned in the second bedroom in their apartment - so in the middle of the night he was hammering support slats into an iron bed to stabilize it after it had fallen when they got into it.] Even though she didn't have profound experiences to draw from, she had significant meaning in her days and her strength in her faith. So much that she wrote poems not about vacation but how heaven will be like a vacation.

A Vacation
There are so many taking vacations to the land, the shores and the sea,
Oh, how I wish they were getting ready to take a vacation with me.
I don't have time for a vacation, I have too much work to do.
My house needs paint on the walls, and I need carpet on my floors too
But that's alright with me because I have so much more in store.
You see, my Father has chosen a better home for me.
And that's worth so much more.
Oh it is crowds and crowds already there, they are waiting for me
But I don't know when I am going to go because I have more seeds yet to
Oh, I love my Husband, my Family, you people and people everywhere
I even love those people in nations across the sea

FAITH FULL

I want everyone to get ready to take a vacation with me.
I don't know where I may have to go or how much work yet I have to do,
But you just wait and see,
When my work is through, I am going to take a vacation too.
I am going to take my vacation in Heaven, where that pearly gate is going
to open wide, And I'm going to see those streets of gold,
Because I am going to be there inside.
It is a Heavenly choir there that is going to sing sing that so many is not
going to be able to sing
But I am going to be there with them, because my Father us there,
And He is the King.

This house is never locked, and everyone is welcome if they can get through
the door.
For your see, they are going to have a lot more in store.
My father is there setting on the throne,
And when I get there I am going to love and welcome everyone into my
Home
For in my Father's house there are mansions that many has not yet seen.
Now let me tell you are going to have everything.
We will never go hungry, for you see He is the King.
My, I haven't been used to having everything,
When I get there, I am going to feel like a queen.
Now, if you should go before I do, that is alright too.
For everything is ready and waiting for you.
Just make yourself at home.
And when my work is through, I will be coming home,
Then I will be with you.
Now what is the expense for this vacation?
The price has been paid all the Way.
All you have to do now is really know the truths.
Then you can see the light, then there won't be no doubt in what is the Right
Way.
Yes, there is so many taking vacations to the land, the shore, and the sea

Let us pray that everyone will get ready, so when their work is through
That they can take a vacation with <u>me</u> and <u>you</u>.

Arletta M. Clutteur June 24, 1978

The Poem *Vacation* came to her while she was preparing a meal in her kitchen. She heard a beautiful choir singing and tried to turn the radio up, but the radio was not on. To say she was motivated to write isn't necessarily true, either. She just sat down after realizing the profoundness of her experience, opened her heart and her pen cap, and felt the love and the Lord flow out of her. This was her gift and her service to her Creator.

Both her and Jim did not expect any recognition or even a thank you in their motivations to serve. She recalls seeing an honest and caring man anytime she looked at my grandfather. She shared the story about one hot summer he was reflecting on their neighbor's life who didn't have money to spend and my grandfather (pappy, as I called him) bought the neighbor an air conditioner "on time" (which is like lay-away, but where you could take it with you). This was common practice of the 50s-60s because many of the stores knew you well enough or if they didn't, they still trusted you. They bought their bedroom set from a store called Dentons, also "on time" where they made payments regularly. They wouldn't fret over bills because in this simple time, that fostered love and goodness of people, if you didn't have money to make the payment, you'd get in touch with your creditor and work out an arrangement. In small towns back then, your word was as good as bond. The time period as well as the small town all conspired to support kindness and love.

As a young girl, she dreamed of entertaining guests, planning social events and doing things to help those in need. She also discovered a love of singing, which will become another vehicle of love and purpose later when she began recording music and eventually when she had her singing tour business, White Dove Tours. She recorded her first album in the 70s and was immediately appreciated by folks around her for taking something she's so passionate about and creating out of her own ambition.

Tied closely to her motivation to love, and leading with love, is her guiding principle of being not afraid to die. It all bundles together this sense of just going for it, having faith in the Lord and not worrying about when it's her "time" to go. She has had so many ups and downs and close calls with illness as a senior, she remains consistently at peace if it's her time to pass on from this earth. There was only once in her life that she said she's not yet ready and that was during her brush with cancer as a new mom. Every other time it's been a surrender to her maker and an acceptance that she's lived life her best, most purposeful way, and for the glory of God.

Life Poem

What does life really mean?
Is it made up of many different things?
Or is it when we meet far seen things?
For this is Love that God can share,
When we let Him know we do care.

Life is different. It's different every day,
To each of us in a different way.
My life to me, I thought was doing well,
Then came that day when God came along --
He talked to me in my home.
A gift of love, I knew was true.
A new life I may share with you.
But many of my friends think it is not true,
They say "I am sorry. What can I do?"

Oh God, I pray for these friends that a new life in them will soon begin.
A love will grow and life within.
Then they will understand what I'm saying, (sharing)
Through the love of God I found that day.
No one on earth can take away.

White Dove October 25, 1973

It's nearly impossible to have such a life of love without an essence of acceptance. As we'll see in the hardships chapter, most of which did not deter her, still hardships she did have and hardships she did love for the strength they gave her. She recently said that all of life's difficulties prepare her for what's to come (and I also heard my dad say that a few years back when dealing with back to back loss of his life partner and then his brother within a short span - a notion she and Jim must have embodied their whole lives and passed on to their children). But what does acceptance really look like for someone who loves to love? When she was a new mom of three, recovering from a hysterectomy (which today we know can do incredible things to our hormones, something they didn't' know in the late 50s and early 60s), Arletta had an incredible experience that underscores her ability to accept what is… and also to be resilient as her life's training was preparing her for.

It was early one morning when she was outside feeding the dog. Suddenly she felt the earth under her feet get hot. She looked around to see what appeared to be earthquakes and cracks. She could not humanly understand, and she wanted to tell someone about her experience. In her bathrobe, she ran to the neighbor's house. People didn't speak of their visions or anything that might innervate or concern others then, at least in her circles, so the neighbor called her husband who took Arletta to the doctor, who sent her to the hospital. While there, she refused an injection because she feared they would sedate her, and instead screamed, "No! God protect me!" and was soon taken to the jail house. When her husband Jim arrived, she saw the pain in his face and felt it within her own body. She tried to remain strong, but the words that came to her calmly were, "Jim honey, remember when I said a few weeks ago that I thought I was going away? I didn't know where at the time, but now it's clear, that premonition was that I was going to be committed at Western State Mental Hospital. When you asked where I was going, I said you will know when the time comes. Then, a week ago, I saw bars in a second vision. And now here I am, going to Western State. You can lock me up, but I know Christ is with me and will give me the strength and courage." While this was not a proud moment for her life story, it was one she would never trade. She says it was a life experience that no money could ever buy. While there, Arletta explained she felt the presence of the divine. She felt at ease and even excited. The professionals believed she was suffering from schizophrenia and was left under evaluation for several days.

While there she saw things that no one often sees in a lifetime. A woman came up to her and said, "if I had a knife I would stab you." Arletta's response was classic and embodies the acceptance illustrated n this chapter. She said "well it might not hurt all that much right now, but I love you" while looking the woman deeply in the eyes. Arletta continued, "when I look in your eyes I see the stars." A few days later, Arletta washed and curled the lady's hair. She befriended the lady with her love and acceptance, as she did with many during her time there.

The review board asked her if she was proud of herself. Her reply was so sharp and observant and turned the question on them. They ended up releasing her, but not before she promised to bring some of her resident friends to her house. And she did. On June 16, 1980 a busload of inmates and staff came, listened to a band play music and enjoyed each other outside the confines of the hospital. When she returned home, a letter from Jerusalem had arrived. She left it for her husband to see at the dinner table. He simply cried and took the letter with him - she hasn't seen the letter since.

Still moved by what she experienced inside the hospital, and the divine gifts many of the residents had (seeing messages from their Creator, having a mental acuity that she had not come upon before in others), Arletta hosted a busload of residents again back at the Friendly Grove at Bennett's Run for a picnic in 1985. Restaurants and businesses, as well as family and friends helped make it possible for the table to be filled with food.

While no one really spoke of it until I came along and started asking questions, Arletta is proud to be able to survive what would have been a defining moment for many and pivot her experience into helping others.

This is her coping mechanism: recognizing that she has plenty of gifts and relative to others and is very fortunate. Rather than feel stymied by events that happen to her, she finds a way to see beauty, opportunity or the lesson, and in this lesson – one of life's most important, is that that everyone needs to feel love, especially those in need.

Flowers and Friends

Did you ever look at a flower and compare it to
a friend? As I looked at you that's what I
did, a flower stands out with beauty then it
will fade away, but the beauty if that memory
will live on from day to day. For you see we
belong to Jesus he's our friend and we are
his flowers, we never know when it's time for
picking, it could be in an hour if the hour should
come quickly there's no need to fret for there will
be many memories left behind to live on from day
today. Where you see Jesus picked another
flower for his big bouquet.

By Arletta Clutteur

When being interviewed for this book, she offered without being pressed for specific wisdom, "Never give up. Be thankful for each day regardless of the challenge. We are blessed and the breath we breathe is a gift." Yes, her positivity and gratitude is hard-wired. Yet, no matter the motivation, religious or not, if it comes from a place of goodness, I believe it's sustainable. Using Arletta as an example, we can all try to be more benevolent, more compassionate, and orient with love and service. I believe the results will look like hers and offer a much more fulfilling life.

Chapter 3: Hardships

One swallow does not make a summer.

Being born in the late 30's brought with it a level of difficulty unique to its era, especially in the hills of Bergton, Virginia. There was a sugar ration and during this time, you needed to have stamps to buy food. Arletta's mother would fashion clothes out of printed cotton bags and made petticoats out of flour sacks. Arletta's family lived up a big hill in a hollow mountain on both sides, so much that the school kids would make fun of Arletta that she'd need one short leg to always traverse those hills. She never took anything seriously - her reply, "I got one long leg and one short leg but, I get around, don't I?" And the teasing did not stop her from racing the hills regularly. Neither did the fact that her family was incredibly poor, even in a time of global hardship and difficulty. She only knew her world and the world just over that mountain was even worlds away. Her biggest worry was bears. The neighbor kids knew it and would hold her back so she would have to run home by herself. Even recalling that today sees how the kids were playing and didn't let it define her as a victim or motivate her to prove herself to others.

She also didn't realize what she was missing in an absent father. Her mother did her best to make up the difference, and never spoke of his alcohol addiction or refusal to want to be a part of her world. She offered so much love and stability that even when Arletta learned that her father said some terrible things about Arletta as she was being born, despite the pain from her natural desire to be loved, Arletta still knew she was lovable. He had not even met Arletta when her mother Elva was labouring slowly with the midwife. When she told Elva's husband that they would need to see the doctor, that either the mother or the baby would not make it, his response was that he would "rather see a baby die than a lamb." Arletta learned of this story much later from a relative of that midwife. Alas, she rationalize that any hate in his heart that drove him to these choices would certainly not be the sentiment she felt in her own heart, even for a man who didn't share the same love.

A CONTINENT

God created a Continent of Glory filled it with treasures untold.
He carpeted it with soft-rolling prairies and vast deserts, towering pine-
clad mountains and magnificent valleys.
He adorned it, with sweet-flowing springs and traced it with winding
streams and rivers that flow in the seas.
He planted the deep-shadowed forests and filled them with song,
and to beautify, he added flowers, their fragrance freshens the air like
perfume.
Then He called thousands of people and summoned the bravest among
them, they come from the ends of the earth, each bearing a gift and a
hope to a remote continent.
If it be in a hollow on a mountain in a valley prairie, desert or on the
sea, they battled against fear and proverty the blend of old and new
of work and faith.
The glow of adventure was in their eyes and in their hearts the glory
of hope, and out of the loning hearts and prayers of the souls, God
formed a nation in love blessed with a purpose sublime and we
called it America The Beautiful

(A Friend-AC 1/30/88-8/28/88)
White Dove

The early settlers - to them America was a New World. We, the New Generation, think of America as Liberty, a Land of Freedom and Opportunity.
America first appeared on a map in 1507. To refer to the United States of America (A Lone) (Info. from New Standard Encyclopedia)

While this focus on the love she did have is a mature and healthy approach to rejection, the truth is, this young heart did always wonder why her father would abandon her. She knew he had his own troubles that had nothing to do with her or her mother, knew that her mother was in a much happier place with her new husband Charlie. Arletta asked God to forgive her dad as He had forgiven her, a sinner saved by grace. She learned much of this giving her woes to god from her mom, who coped with her situation but never expressed hate. Arletta believed that God would forgive her father one day so it was not for her to judge him or have ill feelings towards him. But the logic does not rationalize away the loss, and Arletta did not avoid her feelings when reflecting on her father. She has known loss her whole life. Despite that her family worked so hard to show her unconditional love, she also was mature enough to see their effort here. She embraced loss, surrendered to her Lord and adopted the mantra that all of this pain is here to evolve her and teach her to cope with the next wave of feelings. While a devout Christian, this philosophy is a very Buddhist one. It's universal in love and growth in that with the strength in believing in a higher being, you can face all things thanks to your divine plan. This Universal understanding was passed from Arletta and Jim onto their children, as I overheard my own father use this in coping with the losses later in his life. This helped her live through so much hardship: her own diagnosis with cancer, the hole in the heart of her youngest son when he was born (recovered), a motorcycle accident of her eldest son Jim Jr, a broken back plus six heart attacks, a stroke, and ultimately death by cancer of her husband, Jim Sr, and the death of one of her children, several siblings and her teen niece and middle-aged nephew.

Even equipped with philosophy and the Lord's plan, losing her first husband Jim Sr. was a slow and painful process. A few years after the launch of her tour business, the diagnosis and deterioration began. Even though he insisted on her continuing on the tours as he knew how much joy taking seniors on trips brought her, she felt conflicted and torn, even on day trips when he would still be healthy enough to work, care for himself and so on. She also needed to continue keeping her hours at Wal-Mart to continue the benefits available to her ailing spouse. Add these extra feelings to the uncertainty and feeling the pain he was feeling for having been together for so long, Arletta regards this as one of the most difficult periods in her life. My memory of grandma during this time was that she was quieter seemed to not tell as many stories about the beauty of the world she's observed or has been revealed to her in her dreams. This was her grieving the man she loved and trusting in one as He takes the other from her. This is a conflict so many Christians face but must have been critically hard for Arletta as she moved straight from living at home, taking care of her little brothers and sisters to taking care of a husband and soon to be family at the age of 16. While her mother and stepfather would live long lives and die while Arletta's children were grown, the experience of death would not become real until her "Jim Honey" was about to meet their maker. Even in her own close call, fighting and overcoming ovarian cancer shortly after the birth of their third child at the age of 26, facing impermanence never crossed her mind then because she had so much work to do. Both for her family and for her time on this planet, she believed it wasn't her time and prayed she would see her children grow up. But she couldn't be so irreverent when facing the death of her spouse when she was in her 60s. She never questioned her Lord's plans for this man but did share with me that she didn't know what she was going to do when he was gone. My grandfather fought long and hard for his "Mama Baby" but in the end, the cancer won and he left this earth on November 20, 2003. Arletta recalls looking out his hospital window and the landscape looked golden. She leaned in and told him what she saw, a street of gold, which was a way he ended his prayers when teaching Sunday School earlier in life (he would say, "when our life on this earth is done, may we all walk that street of gold."). She told him it was okay to go, and just in that moment, her friend pointed out a rainbow that was also out his window. "With God as her witness," two doves also took flight in this scene of rainbows and sparkles of gold, and with this backdrop, my grandfather took his last breath. She again saw signs from her Lord that this is all his divine plan and while that didn't make the pain of the loss go away, it did deepen her trust in the Lord.

Rainbows and Roses

Rainbows and roses, this is love
Rainbows and roses, I know who makes them both.
Everywhere I go each day, the love I share along the way,
Rainbows and roses this is love.

I was sitting in my home one day, talking to a friend
And he looked at me strangely, this is what he said,
"White Dove, it's a rainbow, there about your head."
I smiled, and this is what I said:

Rainbows and roses, this is love
Rainbows and roses, I know who makes them both.
Everywhere I go each day, the love I share along the way,

FAITH FULL

Rainbows and roses this is love.

If your day is dark and sun you cannot see,
Turn your thoughts toward heaven
And a touch of love
God in all His glory, his love it will flow free,
A message of love from our king.

Rainbows and roses, this is love
Rainbows and roses, I know who makes them both.
Everywhere I go each day, the love I share along the way,
Rainbows and roses this is love.

As you travel the road of life with doubters along the way
Always think positive in what you do and say
If you meet someone in need, reach out a loving hand,
A friendly smile upon your face, they will understand.

Rainbows and roses, this is love
Rainbows and roses, I know who makes them both.
Everywhere I go each day, the love I share along the way,
Rainbows and roses, this is love.

Written in 1984, the words are explained in the song and is by far one of Arletta's most popular songs.

Thirteen years later she would experience another significant loss, this time the loss of her eldest son, Jim Jr. Jim was a truck driver and would spend a lot of time on the road, but he would always come visit his mother when he was coming back into town after hauling loads each week. Once day a few weeks before his vehicle accident, he shared with her he gets to see God's glory every morning with the sunrise. He shared with her a vision he had (he was not known to have the same visions of his mother, but this time was different) of a bridge passing over into heaven. Before this conversation, Arletta wasn't really sure where her eldest son's faith was. She did her best to teach her children about Jesus and share openly her experiences to encourage them to enjoy the gifts of the Lord, but as adults, they didn't really go deep into the subject. Until this particular day when Jim Jr. shared his vision. He wanted to talk about it with someone, and she was honored to be that person. She was also affirmed that the Lord did have a plan here too because when she received the tragic news a few weeks later, the timing of his conversation with her made so much sense. While it was a terrible loss and she had no time to prepare herself or her family who were also grieving, she knew he was in heaven, and took great comfort in this.

The death of her son came shortly before the death of her later-in-life love, Norvel Fishel. The two met on one of her tours and had similar interests, especially in church and sharing the gospel. He actually resembled Jim Sr. quite a bit and suffered a long death, so Arletta was mentally prepared when his time came. She'd been down this road before and was certain she would see him again in heaven. He showered her with gifts, words of affirmation, acts of service and all the love she could imagine. While she loved my grandfather deeply, Norvel put her on a pedestal and outwardly adored her in a way that made her sparkle even brighter. She shined brighter than I've seen her in this lifetime when he was by her side and a true companion she found in Novel. They would talk about their late spouses, share in gratitude, and enjoyed worshiping together. She was very sad at his passing but continued on the legacy they built together of making apple dumplings and spreading gospel in his honor. She would talk of him and continue to host his family for holidays and carried on as if his presence was still alive and real. This celebration of life and honoring of the legacy is something Arletta knew well in all of the benefits she's organized in her lifetime and even when it was time to grieve for the people who influenced her life as well.

While loss of loved ones are among the hardest to bear, Arletta's loss story doesn't end there, Hardships can and do turn into opportunities to evolve, if you let them. A final, yet earlier, example of this was when Arletta was working for Rockingham Poultry in 1985, she heard first what sounded like a trumpet. She asked someone nearby if they heard it, too. Then it turned into a terrible rumble in her ear - as if a train were near her head. She went to the doctor only to find that her eardrum had not only ruptured but she would need to have immediate, reconstructive surgery on the bones in her ear to have any chance at hearing. Arletta declined because this would be the weekend the residents of Western State would be hosting them at a picnic at Bennett's Run. Mind you, Arletta had no real money to offer, but setting a table for them was in her vision and the show must go on, and many restaurants and sheriff's officers were standing by to help pull off this event. Against doctor's orders, she delayed the surgery for another week.

While she eventually did resume hearing in that ear, it was a long road to recovery. When she was debriefing with the doctor, he explained that her eardrum was totally missing. The shape of the bones in her ear were like nothing he's seen. He even drew a picture to show the very unique scenario he saw when repairing her ear. The doctor was able to restore her hearing against tremendous odds. What's also interesting is when he took the bandage off her ear, the blood clot in the bandage was in the shape of a heart, with the symbols alpha and omega around. She takes this as a message from her Lord and believes this doctor not only restored her hearing but also her ability to tune into the messages she receives from God.

Later in life at the same job in 1998, a fire extinguisher exploded near her and she inhaled the dust particles deeply into her lungs. She would suffer for many years, be permanently hoarse, require years of speech therapy and eventually give up singing, but look back to that fateful moment, just like the ear incident, often. She may have permanent damage from this incident but remains positive. She never told the story woefully, but rather, found examples of the Lord even in those hardships and didn't let them define her. All of these stories of hardship validate her.

Part II

"Echo"

As I stood upon that mountain
Down in the valley that day
I heard an echo come through
This is what the echo did say

I love you, I love you
I love you, I love you
Regardless where you may be
If it's on the highest mountain,
On this valley, or across the sea.

While my journey's beginning,
I don't know where it might lead.
I'm looking forward friends, to meeting you
In our garden someday.

I love you, I love you
I love you, I love you
Regardless where you may be
If it's on the highest mountain,

On this valley, or across the sea.

The storms they are a raging,
Many we've already seen
But let us all get ready
That someday we all may sing

I love you, I love you
I love you, I love you
Regardless where you may be
If it's on the highest mountain,
On this valley, or across the sea.

Strange words I have spoken,
Many do not understand me.
Someday they'll see an echo
That's living in me each day.

I love you, I love you
I love you, I love you
Regardless where you may be
If it's on the highest mountain,
On this valley, or across the sea

© 1974 Arletta M Clutteur

Song written in 1974 and was inspired by an experience at the Friendly Grove/Bennett's Run where others had gathered to hear a worship service. Her eldest son noticed some moisture in the ground and began to dig. He dug until the spring bubbled up and an elderly man asked the Reverend to baptize him there that day in the unearthed spring. The joy she and others experienced felt like an echo in the mountains, and thus the song was born.

Arletta and Jim Sr with the cake he had made for her birthday

Chapter 4: Impact

"A bird does not sing because it has an answer. It sings because it

has a song." - Maya Angelou

Some schools of thought are that you spend a lot of time learning, then you do. Or, spend a lot of time practicing, then you perform. Then there are the folks who believe you just go for it… that you never know until you try. While chance does often favor the prepared, it favored the "motivated by goodness" in the case of Arletta. She did not know much about literature before she began writing poems. In fact, she knew little about writing in general because she left school before she was 16. She was planning to return to school the fall before she met my grandfather and her life took a different turn. She had her sack dress ready to go and had saved enough money to cover the costs associated with going to school from her summer babysitting job. However, when she saw that her younger siblings didn't have coats to wear, she decided to send them to school, using her earnings for the necessary attire instead.

When asked about what her favorite subject in school was (before she dropped out), she said she liked spelling. Perhaps this enjoyment of the subject helped her confidence when she began writing poetry and songs, but she would argue that it was the strong current of love and believing she had messages from God that pushed her past any insecurities of not having training to do what she believed was her passion and purpose for that moment.

She also never had any formal musical instruction yet has written and recorded several songs and poems. In the early 70's she recorded "Labor of Love: Poems and Songs by White Dove."

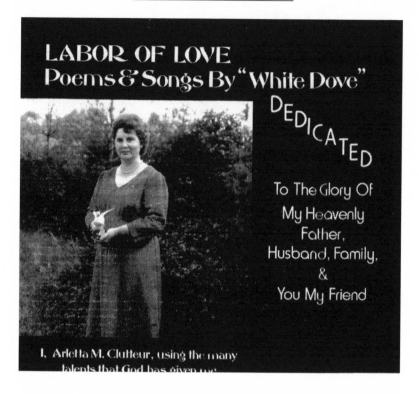

Arletta's first album cover from the mid 1970's

She went on to perform onstage in Ocean City, Maryland and in Wheeling, West Virginia. She later recorded a compact disc (CD) of her music and poems called "Soaring on the Wings of the Dove." While she needed to take a loan for the $2,000 to produce this CD, her husband was supportive. He said, "when the Lord speaks, you listen." This CD was sent to Jerusalem in 2014 where she received a letter of acknowledgement thanking her for her symbol of peace.

Arletta loved to write and even her letters are often like prayers. She recognized her creative talents and channelled them into poetry early on when writing the poem for Bennett's Run in the early 70's but that was only the beginning. With each poem or song she was delighted, energized, and propelled to write more. There isn't a day you don't hear Arletta humming a tune or reciting one of her poems. When asked where her inspiration comes from she responds, "it just comes to me." If you press a little further, she always harkens back to a sign or some omen from the Lord that motivated her to share these messages, like the time a heart appeared on her arm on August 4, 1984. The heart was a bruise with no explanation other than the Lord was trying to get her attention. Once she was done, these poems never went in a book or a box. They were printed, displayed as reminders, or most often, given as gifts to others. Even though she never set out to write a poem or song specifically for a head of state or the president, she would think of them, then a theme would come through to her. She knew the finished product, whatever form it was, was meant to be sent along. And listen to her heart, she did, and has an entire safety deposit box of responses from country leaders thanking her for her prayers, her talents and for sharing so much hope and observations of beauty with the world. When asked about these noble gestures, she simply responds, "you can send a message without a riot or a lot of money."

Free will is a topic you hear a lot about in religious circles. Sure, your path may be created for you by God, but there is a choice always there for you to decide to align with the path or not. Arletta was a firm believer of this, and the sentiment has been handed down among the generations (without explicit teaching) because her granddaughters took choices by the reigns and opportunities to ripple out impact, when possible. More on the trickle effect in Chapter 7. It always bothered her when she'd hear that the kids are being just like their parents - that the example was made for them to follow. While this is probably true for behaviors like yelling or fighting, Arletta made sure she chose which patterns she wanted to carry out to the world and which she left behind. This is why she never touched alcohol for the entirety of her life. Because her father was an alcoholic, she believed she had a choice to not become that, so it motivated her to use that energy to become impactful. Not just in poetry but also in enterprise.

Serving you with a smile, a song, and an exciting time

Arletta was an entrepreneur before she knew what it really meant to start a business or create anything. And just like her poetry, she had no training in business, but believed in herself and the opportunity. She created White Dove Tours in 1997 specifically because she saw how many seniors were looking to do something meaningful with their time through her role at Wal-Mart where she would organize weekly bingo games. She approached her boss to see if it would be a conflict of interest (it was deemed no conflict) and incorporated her business. She took these seniors on adventure at least monthly, organizing her registrations via pen and notebook. She would always provide lunch (usually a ham sandwich and chips), ensure of everyone's comfort, and sing songs regularly in the motorcoach, in addition to the little white dove souvenir she would give to guests. With 18-20 tours a year, one of her regulars collected 89 plastic doves before her death some years later. Charlotte Robinson and her husband Richard were regulars on her tours and said she always started each tour with a prayer.

In her dealings, she would occasionally create flyers or brochures advertising an upcoming trip, but most often her buses were booked sheerly from word of mouth. She would negotiate the rate with the tour bus company, work out accommodations with venues and hotels and calculate her costs and margins effectively...all without a single business class. While it wasn't such a huge operation that allowed her to retire in luxury, she enjoyed the small return the business offered and leveraged the success to build an ADA-accessible room on the back of her house, intended to help her and my grandfather to age-in-place. One of her tour guests came to visit her once and was surprised to see what little means she had. The friend's comment was, "Oh I thought you had everything, and you don't even have a dishwasher!" (She still washes dishes by hand in 2021.)

Her biggest benefit, however, was to see her guests and seniors experience joy and wonder in their later years. She loved taking them to new places and even managed a cruise to Bermuda and to Alaska in some of her pinnacle tours. The business was born out of Arletta's love of travel, experiencing new things and ministering to others through music and good fellowship. The name was given by her late husband Jim when she asked what she should call it. He looked at her and smiled while saying "White Dove Tours."

Her most frequent destinations were Christian music and drama performances, often to Renfro Valley, Kentucky and Pigeon Forge, Tennessee. Straight from her brochure, it summarizes the experience: "through her special kind of tours, Arletta continues to sow seeds of love and kindness and be a blessing to others. She hopes to be of service to you, your friends, the community and beyond." This summation was discovered mid-writing of this book, but the quote, captured by her friend Judy Emswiler Williams, summed up a key theme of this memoir, nearly two decades prior: her mission was, and always has been, simple and true. In an interview by the Northfork Journal November 12, 2002, Arletta was quoted saying "All I have to offer is service," and so it was a perfect combination of her purpose, passion and talents. Even though she required help from a friend to manage the tours after an accident at her primary job made it difficult to speak, much less sing, it was a positive chapter for Arletta and she reflects on the experience fondly.

Traveling with Jesus

Wilhelmina Santiful/Valley Herald

Arletta Clutteur of Broadway displays of some of the trips she arranges as owner of White Dove Tours.

White Dove Tours offer travel, fellowship

Wilhelmina Santiful
svh@shentel.net

On her wedding day, Arletta Clutteur's husband, Jim, whispered that she would always be his white dove. This became her nickname, and now it is the name of Clutteur's tour business.

White Dove Tours is a licensed broker offering bus tours and cruises to church groups, organizations, businesses and private groups.

"White Dove Tours, which opened for business in 1997, was born out of my love of travel to experience new things and my desire to minister to others through fellowship," said Clutteur.

"It is important that my guests are comfortable and that they enjoy the trips. My motto is, 'Tomorrow's business will depend on today's service.'"

To guarantee first-class service, Clutteur supervises every detail of the tour arrangements. She escorts each of the 18 to 20 annual trips, which are mostly

luncheon cruise on "The Spirit of Norfolk" – plus a Potomac Eagle train ride to West Virginia are offered this year.

Recent religious tours include those to Sight and Sound Theatre in Pennsylvania to see the biblical play "Ruth," to Living Waters Theatre in Lancaster, Pa. to see "The Psalms of David," to the Mother Church of American Methodism in Baltimore, to Lighthouse Restaurant in Pennsylvania to a gospel concert featuring the Lewis Family, and to the MCI Center in Washington to hear TV minister Joel Osteen.

Other trips have been to National Air and Space Museum at the Steven F. Udvar-Hazy Center at Dulles Airport and to see "Big River" at Riverside Center Dinner Theater in Fredericksburg.

"As a souvenir of my tours, I always present a miniature white dove to my departing guests as a symbol of love, tranquility and unity of mankind," said Clutteur.

"Just last month I received a letter of appreciation from a man

of my tours.

"A former guest, who had been touring with my company since I went into business in 1997, had collected 89 doves before her demise.

"My work in the tour business is truly a labor of love."

More info: White Dove Tours, (540) 896-7457.

Upcoming tours
• Oct. 7 -9 Music Hall of Fame Museum, Renfro Valley, Ky.
• Oct. 22 Country Store Opry in Franklin, W.Va.
• Nov. 11-13 "Christmas in the Smokies," Pigeon Forge, Tenn.
• Dec. 3-4 "Winterfest of Lights" and "Country Christmas Memories," Ocean City, Md.

First Church
of Columbia Furnace

Location: Columbia Furnace Union Church

Worship Service

at 11 a.m.

Article in the Northfork Journal

Some years later, Arletta had trouble getting around due to a pinched nerve in her leg. It became too difficult to properly host the tours, so she decided to close the business in 2015. Like most entrepreneurs, you rarely find anyone who is 'one and done' so she found herself baking ad nauseum her delicious cakes and apple dumplings for the locals, even while still slowly recovering and experiencing pain in her leg. Someone had tasted her goodies from a fundraiser she contributed to and the phone did not stop ringing from there. If there was money given for her goodies, she would cover her costs and donate the rest to her church. As I write this in 2020, she was working on five cakes for pick up, even during a global pandemic (COVID-19) when many folks are trying to stay indoors and not eat in public settings. Here again, she doesn't charge high margins - just enough to cover her costs, mostly. She never charges for her time and says she works so hard baking and producing because it keeps her busy. I imagine it also keeps her purpose alive in that she's able to do something helpful to others with little cost to herself.

It was this purpose that started her on organizing enterprises and baking for goodness back in the 70s. This is probably where her confidence to go for it, willingness to take risks in the name of positive outcomes, and motivation to create something bigger than you all began. In 1972, Arletta had a vision of a table. She wanted to create a place to bring together people, to break bread, and to enjoy the beauty that is around us. On her record album cover, she writes of "A True Labor of Love" and describes the beginning of Bennett's Run reunions. She says "It all began

July 10, 1971… when [she] was walking with her husband…" in the area that would become the home of the annual picnic for years to come. She told him of a vision to have a big meal in honor of these grounds that she grew up in, enjoying her spiritual connection to the Bennett's Run hills. She had already asked her husband to make her a Wishing Well for the area she looked back on so fondly. She wanted to raise money to help restore the area that she had enjoyed as a kid, so set out to create a plan. She would bake a huge cake and sell slices of it to help raise money for the maintenance required for the land. She organized a clean-up of the grove, got volunteers to come play music and provide entertainment, and provided the basic food to feed hundreds of people. In the end, this Bennett's Run Reunion took on a life of its own.

Editorial note: I didn't realize until writing this book that I share the same birthday as the Bennett's Run Reunion (July 10), ten years apart.

Community Reunion

By MARY JANE KING
N R Staff Writer

BERGTON — Traditionally reunions are for renewing old friendships, admiring new babies and feasting on favorite recipes from a long, plank table.

The Bennett's Run reunion held recently provided all the traditional reunion fare plus a few extras.

One of the extras was the setting. The Bennett's Run area can boast some of the most beautiful forest and mountain land in western Virginia.

Remotely situated, about a mile down the mountain from the West Virginia border, it seems almost a miracle that settlers found their way there in the late 1700's.

But it is understandable that those same settlers chose to stay near the run that today bears one of their names.

And though most of their descendants have left the community, they have not lost interest in their past — the 300 people who attended this year's annual reunion are the evidence.

After a huge meal which included at least 15 varieties of potato salad, some of the children took to the mountains to play while the adults exchanged memories of one-room school houses and childhood.

The Bennett's Run School House was built in 1902 on land donated by Sol Smith. The property is now owned by his grandson, Loy. The school closed in 1950.

Two former teachers, Mrs. Eileen Nesselrodt and Mrs. Everett May, were present at the reunion.

Three gospel and country groups provided appropriate entertainment for the occasion. And near the newly-constructed bandstand flew the United States flag, given to the community by the Harrisonburg Woodman of the World.

Late that afternoon people began to say their farewells and collect their children and lunch baskets. And one by one the cars moved slowly along the dusty road by Bennett's Run, passing the site where a trapper named Bennett was killed by an Indian hunting party.

It was the second Bennett's Run reunion, and Mrs. James Clutteur of Broadway is already working on the next one, set for the fourth Sunday of August 1973.

OLDEST GUEST — Perry Hottinger, 90, was the oldest guest at Bennett's Run reunion. Mr. Hottinger was born in Bergton and lives near Harrisonburg. The youngest person at the reunion only four months old.

Article Published in Daily News Record in 1971

While initially perhaps people came for the food, it was the community that was built as a result of this experience that kept them coming back year after year, even as they became grown adults. Eventually because it was a large undertaking, Arletta decided to let the reunion be picked up by the children and grandchildren of the founding attendees and resigned her post. This was also around the time when her family's health conditions continued to challenge everyday life activities, so the decision seemed right to Arletta. Unfortunately, despite an article in the Daily News Record enticing anyone to step forward to take on the role, the reunion was on the brink of becoming extinct. Thankfully, her sisters took the reigns and moved the reunion to the Bergton school, where access and insurance were more reasonable. The last reunion meal under Arletta's supervision was served in thirty years after its inception, in 2002.

A highlight along the Bennett's Run journey was when a trail was created in conjunction with the United States Park Service and businesses in the community. As part of Wal-Mart's community initiatives (including Earth Day and education within their immediate community), it was decided that the Bergton School house (built in 1902) would be a feature of the trail. It was dedicated on October 3, 1999 and was an honor to celebrate the settlers, trappers and Indians and all the history that occurred along the trail. Unfortunately, lack of continued funding and floods impacted the trail and it has not received the attention it once had. But Arletta is still proud of all the people who came together to make it happen.

WELCOME TO BENNETT'S RUN

Join us on the Bennett's Run history trail – an easy quarter-mile hike – as it winds its way through lands reclaimed by nature. Imagine, as you walk, the creaking of a mule's harness as a farmer plows his fields or the clank of rocks as the farmer piles rocks to form a wall.

Now managed by the USDA Forest Service, these lands along Bennett's Run – once used by early pioneers for pasture lands and homesteads – have become forest lands for you to enjoy.

Cover photos: The George May home, located 3 miles from Bennett's Run on private land. The May home, not part of the tour, is typical of the buildings of the mid-1800's and is the best example standing today. Descendants of George May still live in the area; the May name is synonymous with Bennett's Run. The larger photo was taken around the turn of the century; the smaller photo in 1999.

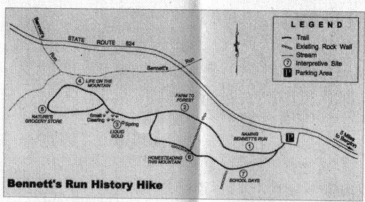

Bennett's Run History Hike

Stops on the Bennett's Run history trail tour are located by number on the map above and described inside this brochure.

PARTNERS IN BENNETT'S RUN HISTORY TOUR

The trail and related publications are products of a Dry River Ranger District partnership with Walmart of Harrisonburg, Virginia, and the Bennett's Run Labor of Love Community Group.

Flyer of the walking trail that was created in partnership with the US Park Service.

FAITH FULL

Bennett's Run

Bennett's Run, O Bennett's Run,
That echoed through the years
The memories we have today are many we can share.
Let us do our work each day
And if the darkened hours of despair overcome us,
May we not forget the strength that comforted us
In the grief of other times,
May we still remember the bright hours that found us
Walking over the silent hills of our childhood,
Or dreaming on the banks of this quiet stream,
When a light glowed within us,
And we promised God to have courage
Amid the changing of the coming years.
Spare us from bitterness
And from the sharp passions of unguarded moments.
May we not forget that poverty and riches are of the spirit.
Though the world know us not,
May our thoughts and actions be such
And shall keep us friendly with ourself.
Lift our eyes from the earth,
And let us not forget the uses of the stars.
Forbid that we do not judge others,
Lest we condemn ourself.
Let us not follow the clamor of the world,
But walk calmly in our path.
Give us a few friends who will love us for what we are,
And keep ever burning before our very steps

The kindly light of hope.
And though age and lack of memory overtake us,
We come not within sight of the castle of our dreams,
Teach us still to be thankful for life,
And for time's olden memories that are good and sweet,
And may evening's twilight find us gentle still,
With memories that echoes through these hills.

In Peace, Love and Beauty
A Friend

© 1971 Arletta Clutteur
This was the first poem Arletta wrote and shared publicly.

The fundraising didn't stop at the church. In fact, one of my earliest memories was for a benefit my grandmother organized for a woman who had been badly burned in a fire. The theme would be heart of the Cherokee Indians and she would have headdresses and costumes created to stage a nativity scene of sorts to encourage people to come donate. She created a whole skit for this (even copyrighted the skit) and said it was a tribute that "peace *is* love." She did a similar benefit for another family who lost everything in a fire. When there was a need, she did what she could to be of service.

Regularly, she would host a meal to raise awareness of church or mission needs, bring community together to enjoy the efforts of the Ruitans impact on the neighbors, and host people in her home for fellowship. She loves cooking as equally as baking but never really taste her product all that much. She says that when she's cooking, she can smell it and it satiates her to the point of not being hungry. Then, if she thinks about eating, it's really the delight in cooking for others that satisfies her so the pleasure of eating isn't there when she eats the food she cooks herself. Ever the host, she loved bringing people together (her favorite meal is not of Italian food but rather "a meal [she] can enjoy with her family"), organizing for a good cause, and making a splash in the name of philanthropy. Even as I write this, she is premaking and sending out 50 meals a month for families under resourced thanks to the global pandemic (COVID-19) of 2020. I called her a few weeks back and asked, "What are you up to?"

"Oh, I'm gonna bake a cake," she replied and then went on to explain that they were for some folks who needed a little sweetness in their day.

When I said, "that's lovely, grandma" her response was simply, "I am just an instrument of love and I do what I can while I still can."

When she was little she dreamed what it might be like to be a tree. Her stepdad had cut down a maple sugar tree and she worked for weeks to dig out the stump. She got down inside the tree pretty far and felt like she was one with the tree. She prayed "God, help me to make my branches grow far and wide." Next, she looked up, there was a man there. Recall this is in the hills of Bergton and you would hear and see someone coming as there wasn't usually traffic on the road.. Still today, there is still a dirt road with not much traffic. Her first words she was able to mumble were "Jesus Christ." Recounting this story today, she is not sure if she learned that phrase as a child or if, perhaps, the man standing there was in fact her Lord and savior, prompting her to use such strong language. She believes so much of her messages from above drive her impact. She doesn't just regard them, she believes in them. Looking back on her life now, she sees symmetry and the recurrence of these messages into themes. She believes the Lord has been talking to her all along, and whatever praise she may receive or impact she may claim, she must give to the glory of God.

Arletta ringing her bell dressed as Mrs. Claus

At some point in the late 70s and early 80s she was inclined to dress up like Mrs. Claus and visit nursing homes to share meals and gospel with the residents. One winter, she was visiting the Farm Bureau where my grandfather was working. He joined in the scene and served as Santa to help delight the children and spread some cheer. Without a plan, they just did as they were called.

All in a day's work of taking care of her community or being a good servant.

Shenandoah Valley

I am pleased to share the beauty I see in this
Shenandoah Valley.

I'm sure I need not tell you of the beauty it offers us.
For in this Valley, with the Mountains roundabout,
Lies a treasure to me there is no doubt.

I think of the Shenandoah Valley as a beautiful garden
With the beauty runabout us.
And the fragrance of the flowers are like perfume
That freshens the air

During the ice storm the Garnder pruned the trees.
Now with the birth of Spring, New Life and Beauty
Blossoms for everyone indeed.

It wasn't planted here for just the wealthy to see,
But also for the humble people like you and me.
Everyone is welcome in this garden, it's beauty if
This they can see
Just for an example look at the flowers and the trees.

By Arletta Clutter - 1978

This poem was written from her hospital window after emergency surgery on an icy eve of Easter. An ice storm had come through overnight and she woke to a glistening scene. She was inspired by the rainbow that reflected from the ice and the sun. The surgery was for a gallstone that looked just like a bird egg, and her husband joked that surely, she was the White Dove after this egg was extracted from her body.

Arletta with a handmade cake for the Ruitans Easter celebration

To show her the heaping stack of all the newspaper articles and appreciation she's received for her effort (this book is just a fraction of the artifacts), she smiles and regards the pictures. She isn't impressed with her own impact but thinks the most fascinating piece of all of her efforts stems from the fact that she really hasn't had much education. All the impact, none of the learnings. Although this is not entirely true. She taught herself throughout life from a 1947 dictionary (still has it, "all taped up") she claims to be a student of the universe and always welcomed the learning, yet didn't let the lack of knowing ever stop her. With a little bit of desire to make the world and her community a better place, and a big bit of faith, she is watching the fruits of her efforts take shape in the love that continually comes back to her in friendship, gifts, and prayers from most anyone who has had the pleasure of knowing grandma.

'Recycled Teenagers' Celebrate Easter

The **Linville-Edom** (VA) Ruritan Club has a reputation for reaching out to senior citizens in the area – primarily because of the passion of one member, Arletta Clutteur, who helps the club host a weekly senior citizen activity at the club building outside Harrisonburg, VA. In April the club and Arletta went above and beyond with an Easter Brunch that brought in over 80 seniors or as they call themselves "Recycled Teenagers." Before 9 a.m. on the third Tuesday of April, the parking lot was full of cars and the seniors inside the building were being led in song. Then the group played a number of rounds of bingo for small prizes and just before lunch a musical duo, Richard and Rita, from nearby West Virginia performed.

Club treasurer and past Rockingham District Governor Jeff Roadcap (pictured center assisting with meal set up) said of Arletta, "She is awesome! She gives so much to others and asks nothing in return. She is the glue which keeps the Recycled Teenagers going. I don't know how many years they have been going but it is definitely a highlight during the week for many of the attendees. The Linville-Edom Ruritans are fortunate to have a few of them as Ruritans as they tend to be very reliable and fun to work with."

The food for the fabulous meal was donated from around the area and included contributions from: Walmart, Golden Corral, KFC, I-Hop, Spanglers, three area Food Lion stores, Costco, BQ Ranch, Lowes, and Flowers Bakery. Decorations, table arrangements and door prizes were provided by Blue Ridge Florist, and Rodamers Landscaping. Not

only did Arletta organize all the food donations and the day's event, she personally made hundreds of small chocolate Easter eggs and a beautiful cake. (pictured at left)

Flowers Bakery donated food items. Party City donated the balloons with messages.

Chapter 5: Living Legacy

Lonesome Dove

When grandma learned I was writing this book for her, she had loads of pictures ready for me. She wasn't expecting a book, but she was hanging onto all of the artifacts that helped explain these unique and profound messages she was receiving throughout her lifetime. The heart of stone was just the beginning, but the stack includes pictures of the face of Jesus looking out bus windows, crosses inside of fresh potatoes she's cut shortly after asking for a sign from God, and many other wild observations that only someone so attuned to beauty and the conversation with God could find.

Heart of Stone

Many times I tried to share a heart of love

Here and there, the more I tried, the less

It seemed that no would call His name.

In my heart His love began to grow and the

Seed, I tried to sow.

My heart of love, my husband and family

Knew but this was not enough for me. I

Had to go in the mountain to search and

See, I was not searching very long,

Before I found my heart of stone. It was though

It was waiting there for me, a heart of stone

That I could see. I knew this was something,

That was real and true. I had to do more than just

Talk about it to you.

God explained it all to me, and on this heart

Of stone He could let you see. The moss He

Planted on this stone, a mushroom also, it was

Standing alone. God told me what to do. And how

I should explain it all to you.

The mushroom represents the life He shares. The moss is

Tenderness, to let us know He cares. The flowers

That you see is the beauty He gave to me.

The dove represents peace and love. Peace among

All nations, and above peace within yourself.

In this heart of stone, I can see, the love of God

Was explained to me.

By Arletta M Clutteur

© September 10, 1973

When I asked her what it's like being a strange bird, or someone responsible for translating these messages of beauty and love, she responds "I'm a nut and that's what's what!" At first, I was concerned that her ability to bypass all the criticism and hardships had gone literally to her head… that it was a survival mechanism still in full gear. But as the years have passed and as the new signs keep coming to her, I truly believe in her case the mind focuses on what it knows and what we practice gets stronger. For her, it's validation of her path on this earth through all these omens and messages from God. She holds fast to a quote she shared as I was compiling this for her: "people think I'm crazy but I know what's in store." And that is how she's gone through life. And how I know she's not really crazy because she's aware of the perception she may have, but simply does not let it phase her. She truly has no pain or regrets. When interviewing her for this book, she shared that over the years people would say things about her strangeness, especially when the messages of God were coming through and she was putting herself out there for the world to feast upon her poetry and music. She worried for her kids and anything that uncomfortable neighbors or friends may say to them. But ultimately, she prayed, "Father forgive them, the truth will be known one day and the truth will set us free." And freedom is what she aligned with when she accepted that she was in fact gifted with ability to communicate with her creator and let Him handle worries like other's discomfort and fears.

What a life, to be free of those burdens. Surely, the strangeness was likely hardwired from the time she was small, but to think that most of us harden as we journey through our experiences, if Arletta has adapted, it has been to become an even larger "instrument of love" and one that scatters peace so freely that it truly doesn't matter who she's offending. Sure, she taught her family to be respectful but she also, through her example, taught us to hold fast to our beliefs and to trust our instincts because they're guided from a source much bigger than us.

Even in her rare-birdness, she still managed to have friends (more than I could ever count/keep track of in her storytelling) and hold respectable jobs. One of her fondest memories was in fact stemming from a unique opportunity she received from working in Wal-Mart as a greeter. She was called into the manager's office. Thinking she was in trouble, she tried to clock out for this discussion. She was told not to. She was also told she was selected to represent the district by attending the annual conference in Bentonville Arkansas, where she would attend along side 20,000 employees and leaders of the company. She called my grandfather to get his thoughts because she had never travelled that far before. He said, "don't let the door close behind you - take this opportunity, Mama Baby." She first wanted to refuse this offering because she felt unqualified. After coming back from the award ceremony, she felt differently. She finally took a breath and realized all of her hard work meant something and was being recognized. While her initial push back was that she didn't even have a high school degree, and they may want to send someone more 'educated,' after she came back she proudly said "I may not have a degree on the wall but I am a graduate of the universe." Following on this opportunity, she was later invited to Richmond, Virginia to receive a "Take Pride in America" award, where awards were handed out by the govenor's wife, and Arletta was still honored to receive such recognition.

Imagine what life would have been like for Arletta if she ignored the messages or denied what was stirring inside of her? Imagine a person with such drive for goodness, a heart full of joy and an imagination to dream up the most extravagant of solutions to problems she sees - imagine what her mindspace would look like if she didn't create these outlets to share. Imagine if all of us could align with our heart spaces and make the impact the little children inside of us years to, be it in our homes, in our communities, in our ripples of legacy we push to the world around us.

Jim Sr, Lyndsey and Arletta Clutteur, 2002. Photo Credit unknown

Part III

"A Mother for A Nation"

Oh God, I thank you for our Nation,
And Nations everywhere.
And especially for those nations, through you,
that love and care.

As a child, I didn't understand about my brothers and sisters
in other lands.
Now God, I've grown older - a mother as you can see.
I can understand so clearly, what those nations mean to me.

Thank you God for caring for a soul like me,
Of all that you have given, I thank you most for my family tree.
You loved and nourished it, and helped the branches grow
Now the branches have changed, this you know.

Help me to understand if the branch should fall,
It will not lose it's beauty.
But as a tree, will stand tall.
Each nation shall stand tall, maybe stand alone.

All you again, I will call to help it be strong.
But if a storm should strike and it starts to fall,
Oh God, please protect it so as a tree it will stand tall.

For when a family tree is weakened, every branch is hurt, be it large or
small
Give that tree knowledge that you really care.
And although a storm may strike it,
A mother's love and understanding she will share.
*© **1974 Arletta M Clutteur***

Written in 1974 after Arletta dreamed she was walking in the White House
in Washington, D.C. While the dream was nothing out of the ordinary as it
was of her in an empty room, she woke up with a troubled spirit. She knew
she needed to get a message to president Nixon. She managed to get the
number to the White House and made contact with an aide. Just as she hung
up the phone, her thoughts went to the news and she turned on the TV just
as the news broke about Watergate. While Arletta does not claim to have
any clairvoyance or special gifts, she knows the Lord speaks to her and uses
her songs to convey the wisdom that her heart is open to sharing.

Chapter 6: New Trees Sprout from Birds' Seeds

Effects of peace scattered

When Arletta was in her mid 50's, she and my grandfather returned home to find a box on their front porch. Inside was a white dove with the only note being "God's Bird." Clearly a gift from someone who knew how religious the couple was, but no other trace of who it was from or why someone was so inclined to offer the gift. They named the bird "Spirit" and it lived for many years in their front room. This example is just one of probably thousands of random gifts people would leave her, as a gesture of saying 'you've been an example of the Lord's beauty, now enjoy this ____ (fill in the blank).' While "The White Dove" ended up being her mascot and nickname given on their wedding day in 1952 (when "Jim Honey" lovingly whispered in her ear "You will always be my White Dove," and the name stuck). She was given then name because she "was kind" according to her husband, and to the rest of her family and community, she scattered peace. She was such a force that caused so many people to go out of her way to thank her. Maybe that's just what Karma is about - she's gone out of her way to be so generous, perhaps this is what we can enjoy from leading with love and goodness.

Your Wedding Day

As you cruise down the road of life
In blessful love requited
Remember, that you will be a team
A happy pair that God has united.
Right now you are looking forward to the years
of joy you will spend
There will be times of disappointment
There will be joy to share
There will be time to ask forgiveness
From those you hold so dear
Put all these things together is what
You must share, for now you are united, and
Everyone knows you are a happy pair.
May this day of happiness linger through all
Of your years.
Thank God for your blessings, and
This sacred bond.
Together, work hand in hand to
Build a happy home.

With love,
White Dove, © 1973
Arletta wrote this poem reflecting back to her own wedding and was asked to share it for many other weddings over the years.

For others, she would write poems for their wedding days, always bake a cake or some pot pies, and never, not ever, show up empty handed, not to mention all the other major events she would organize to help raise money or help in some way. This kindness was always paid forward and you could actually see the ripples her actions would put into motion.

I know for myself, the volunteerism and drive to help others I find myself needing to satisfy comes from her. Both of my parents worked (very hard) and didn't have a lot of time for community or civic involvement. I wouldn't have adopted this behavior were it not for her as I was also a busy student and didn't know how to make extra time for delighting others, but like Arletta, it's in my DNA so I found a way. I also take note of things that come through to me. Whether it be ideas to help others along on their journey or to get unstuck in a situation. I don't know that these are solutions that my brain has manifested, but rather, they seem to have a current of wisdom that is greater than my own creation and I assume the Universe is using me as a conduit, as well. While my faith isn't specifically in the stories of the bible, it is in God and also believe that everything is for a reason.

Another way my grandmother's seeds have been planted in me is that whenever I see a person (or animal) suffer, be it emotionally or physically, I am moved to help them. I do believe I was born this way and it was in my DNA but also nurtured through her and my grandfather's examples passed to their own children and to me.

For my sister, the desire to host gatherings and invite a community to enjoy each other and delicious food, came from her example. She also learned how to think about others from Grandma Arletta's modelling. She distinctly recalls the fundraiser grandma held for a lady who was badly burned in a car accident. Not only the motivation to look out for the less fortunate, but my sister Amanda also decided to pursue a career in biology and pharma after being brought along for the fundraisers for victim of a housefire.

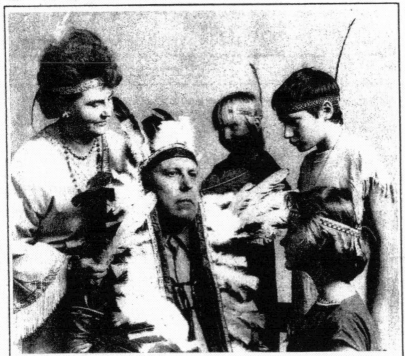

20   DAILY NEWS-RECORD, Harrisonburg, Va., Friday, December 5, 1986

News-Record Photo by Michael Reilly

Preparing For Benefit

Arletta Clutteur and her husband, Jim, and their Three Little Indians rehearse for a skit they will perform at a fund-raiser Saturday for burn victim Krista Smith. The skit, "Tribute to Peace Is Love," was written by Mrs. Clutteur, who also is known as White Dove. The Three Little Indians are the Clutteur's granddaughters, Lyndsey Clutteur and Amanda Shipe and nephew Donald Wilkins. The benefit, which also will include an auction and gospel and country music, will begin 6:30 p.m. at Linville-Edom School. Money from the event will go to Miss Smith, who was burned over two-thirds percent of her body in an auto accident last July.

Article in Daily News-Record featuring the Tribute to Peace is Love skit Arletta designed for the benefit of raising funds for a girl who was badly burned in a house fire.

For her surviving two sons Charlie and David, the 'willingness to do whatever it takes' clearly comes through in their existence. They readily care for their families and her, and there is no question that they'll show up for you. As mentioned earlier, her second son, my dad, has also adopted from her and Pappy the attitude that all of life's experiences prepare us for the next thing. A powerful lesson that they passed along to their children just through their example.

One friend and long-time bus tour follower Charlotte Robinson took the time to let me know that Arletta's love is very much reciprocated. She said, "Arletta's heart and home are always open to everyone."

Fellow volunteers at the time I write this find her inspirational. As I was working with grandma on Martin Luther King, Jr Day in 2021 with the final edits, two beautiful souls from my grandma's network began filing in with food from a nearby food pantry's overflow reserves. I asked what the plan was, and she said that she will either can the goods for delivery (there's 26 families she passes food onto as a septuagenarian herself) or share the bounty with others to help make their grocery bill a little lighter. This is the Ministry of Meals network she's currently an instrumental member of. Between efforts her church does, or her friends Russell and Linda Smith, Arletta is involved with feeding over twenty-six families in her community. While she refuses to take any credit, but everyone in her reach both on the giving and receiving side would agree she's an inspiration in making something good come of these would be discarded goods.

Strangers have commented on what a remarkable woman Grandma Arletta is, just in her presence and the light she brings to a room. She is effervescent and inspirational, even before she opens her mouth.

Arletta's creation for Bingo/Recycled Teenagers Group; Photo Credit Unknown

Many would say she's often evangelical, but even in her messages, she does not push people. She says what she feels compelled if given an opportunity to witness to someone but respects them and doesn't judge them for their opinions or responses to her messages. This is true both of religion and politics. Even in 2020, a year of division and turmoil, she gracefully states her views and beliefs and encourages dialogue, but doesn't push her politics or views on anyone, including her family. She says she's praying for us   and   that   is   all.

Chapter 7: A Bird, came down the walk

(full poem by Emily Dickinson)

"Where flowers bloom so does hope." — Lady Bird Johnson

Being an instrument of love has never been a burden for Arletta. All the messages that have come through are her blessing, even some of the scarier premonitions she's had. Perhaps it was her personality that delights in beauty, or the simplicity in the era she was able to shine in that made her specialness something to behold rather than something heavy to carry. Or, as I reflect on her life and impact, I believe it was a combination of a girl who didn't trouble herself with anything other than love, purpose and faith.

In 1985, Arletta wrote Labor of Love, an Autobiography with the help of a reporter because at that point, she, and the world around her, was already sensing her life was not one that would be left undocumented. But since then, so many more signs from above have come to validate her path and what she's supposed to be doing. She survived cancer and emergencies that many during this time may not have been so blessed to overcome. She did and in the past 35 years, she's been taking these signs for all they have to show her and doing something with her life.

Her primary hope is that she has left behind the seeds that will grow one day, not just for children but for people she's met. Whenever asserting that statement (as I've heard her say a few times now), she follows up that "[she is] not perfect - I'm on this earth so I am not going to be perfect, but this is where the love of Christ comes in."

Dolly Parton, the country singer I grew up listening to, reminds me a lot of my grandmother, not just because of their bubbly, carefree attitudes but she too, feels called to minister through her work. In a podcast interview with Brené Brown, Dolly said, "God works through things like [song writing]; if you have a gift and you're open you can get those messages out to people." She wasn't afraid to tell a hard story in her life and neither is Arletta.

Whether it be motivated by love, helping her community or in sharing her talents, Arletta never wanted recognition because she saw all of her work as an extension of God. Anytime someone offered her a compliment, she always said "if you see any good that I've done, give Him the glory." And while we're on the gift topic, when pressed for her most prized gift, she first recalled bread and milk from her husband when they thought they had no money (he picked up bottles on his way home and sold them to provide these). She later remembered the year that all of her boys conspired to create special deliveries for their mom. The youngest created a ceramic heart, the middle sent one candle brass stick from service (he couldn't afford the second) and the eldest sent a Madonna statue to his mom so she could have a mother on Christmas. She still has each of these items, cherished, and has collected all of the gifts and artifacts people have given her for her generosity over the years.

While her biggest assets in this life are those simple gifts, her biggest accomplishment was hard to narrow in on. She's accomplished a lot in eight decades, starting from when she built tables out of rocks as a child as an omen for tables she'd host to share in community and the gift of life. But when pressured to answer the question, she said that her biggest accomplishment is being able to realize what Christ was doing though her. Recognizing that God had directed her life and doors were opening and any of the accolades or achievements she had were by divine design and recognizing this was pivotal in her lifetime. She hasn't shared too much about all of the pieces of her story broadly, especially the letters from presidents because she felt people didn't want to hear about it. But I did, and I believe others can be inspired by knowing about her walk on this planet.

As I was putting the finishing touches on this book in November of 2020, grandma had a health scare. Her larynx spasmed in the middle of the night and she had a profound experience as images came up when she couldn't breathe and had the most vivid sensations in her throat. She was having a conversation with God while this was going on. Flashes of children in crisis came to her and she prayed "Lord, have mercy on their souls." Then she prayed that if this was her time, she understood, but then prayed "Lord have mercy on me as an earthly being." At that moment she was able to gasp for air and live to tell the story. When reflecting on the story with her doctor, she comments on her near-death experience that "[she is] winning either way."

Her spirit is simply brighter than average. When asked "What's going on, anything exciting?," her response is consistently "Oh, everything is exciting!" and goes into a recent story of divine symbols or messages from above, or how it's all coming together now at the end of her life. She believes all of her stories are on purpose.

When it comes down to it, Arletta has led a rich life and nothing about her experiences has related to money or possessions. The dress she wants to wear at her funeral is the dress she wore to her the wedding of her eldest son (Jim Sr.) in 1986 (she refers to it as her vacation dress).

Completely content with what she is and doesn't dream for a future state that includes materialism or being of a certain means or success measure, Arletta was often recognized for the bright light she brought - her remarkable energy she brought to a room. Anyone who meets with her leaves inspired, with a feeling of peace and warmth from her light. This trait of rippling warmth and love is something I hope I can emulate as I consider what all this exposure to my grandmother could do for my life experience.

Photo credit: Guest on Tour

Learning about my grandmother, being able to reflect on the qualities in me that I already have inherited from her, and being able to consciously choose which I want to carry forward with the rest of my time on earth is a true gift. To be able to have these conversations and ask these questions of my grandmother while she is still living, is a complete blessing. She wasn't always prepared for the answers and sometimes asked for more time to respond, but she thanked me for the opportunity to go back in her mind and explore. Yes, it's not often that you get to ask the provoking questions like, *what does it mean to have a full life like this?*

How do exciting times feel when the normal course is so sacred? What happens to all of these artifacts that are even placed in some museums (Jimmy Carter museum, as an example). No matter how quickly she was able to respond, the answers to these all follow the exact same theme when asked: they all tie to connection. Connection to her messages, her purpose, her legacy (even if the letters get discarded from the museum archives as time passes), to each other. And while love was a prominent theme and motivation of her life, upon reflection, it was also connection. And as this book is written, in a time of unprecedented division among the United States, which Arletta is so proud to live in, the country needs to heal. The country needs her vibrations, and any positive ripples to others from her more than ever. We can open to the possibility of being agents of peace, love and rippling joy simply by reading about motivation, inspiration and impact. To heal, we must reconnect - with stories, with mother earth, with each other, and with ourselves through heartful belonging. Through Arletta's example, we can look at our own effort and see the impact as one person. Then, hope the energy is received and invigorates someone else to do what is within their power.

It didn't occur to me that her mantra "Think of today, dream of tomorrow: each day is a new beginning," she is stating this same ripple philosophy. Translated, she is saying that she's trusting in her goodness today and is grateful (today), she hopes she is lucky enough to do lovely things tomorrow; and she gets to choose how she shows up and for what purpose in her new beginning each day. Arletta ends each phone call with this phrase, and it's the perfect way to end a book dedicated to her true, dedicated, and fulfilled experience on earth.

Lyndsey and Arletta 2020. Photo by Brandy Somers Photography

Extra Resources/Appendix

Letters thanking Arletta for prayers and support:

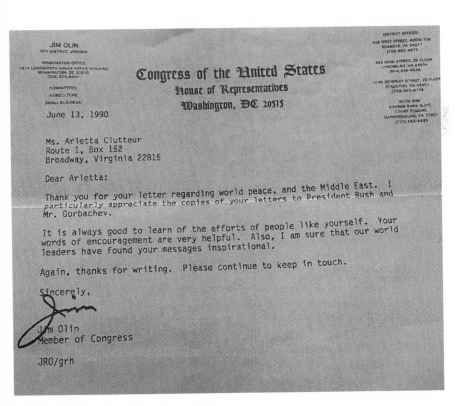

JIM OLIN
8TH DISTRICT, VIRGINIA

WASHINGTON OFFICE:
1314 LONGWORTH HOUSE OFFICE BUILDING
WASHINGTON, DC 20515
(202) 225-5431

COMMITTEES:
AGRICULTURE
SMALL BUSINESS

DISTRICT OFFICES:
406 FIRST STREET, ROOM 706
ROANOKE, VA 24011
(703) 982-4672

925 MAIN STREET, 3D FLOOR
LYNCHBURG, VA 24504
(804) 845-6548

13 W. BEVERLEY STREET, 2D FLOOR
STAUNTON, VA 24401
(703) 885-8176

SUITE 606
SOVRAN BANK BLDG.
COURT SQUARE
HARRISONBURG, VA 22801
(703) 433-8433

Congress of the United States
House of Representatives
Washington, DC 20515

June 13, 1990

Ms. Arletta Clutteur
Route 1, Box 152
Broadway, Virginia 22815

Dear Arletta:

Thank you for your letter regarding world peace, and the Middle East. I particularly appreciate the copies of your letters to President Bush and Mr. Gorbachev.

It is always good to learn of the efforts of people like yourself. Your words of encouragement are very helpful. Also, I am sure that our world leaders have found your messages inspirational.

Again, thanks for writing. Please continue to keep in touch.

Sincerely,

Jim Olin
Member of Congress

JRO/grh

THE WHITE HOUSE
WASHINGTON

August 5, 2010

Dear Friend:

I want to thank you for your message and for holding me in your prayers. My family and I are honored that so many Americans have supported us in this special way.

Our country faces enormous challenges, but each day I am uplifted by the enduring spirit of the American people. I know that we will meet these challenges if our optimism and hope are met with the necessary will and hard work.

We understand that *"the strength to go on produces character. Character produces hope. And hope will never let us down"* [Romans 5: 4-5]. In these times of trial and opportunity, I deeply appreciate your prayers for this country, my family, and myself. May God bless you.

Sincerely,

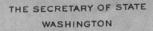

THE SECRETARY OF STATE

WASHINGTON

December 12, 1991

Dear Ms. Clutteur:

I just wanted to send a note of thanks for your
kind letter and banner. I truly appreciate the
special effort you made to write and convey your
warm words of encouragement. Let me assure you
that I deeply value your support.

With best regards,

Sincerely,

James A. Baker, III

Ms. Arlette M. Clutteur,
    Route 1, Box 152,
        Broadway, Virginia.

UNITED NATIONS   NATIONS UNIES

POSTAL ADDRESS—ADRESSE POSTALE: UNITED NATIONS, N.Y. 10017
CABLE ADDRESS—ADRESSE TELEGRAPHIQUE: UNATIONS NEWYORK

REFERENCE

12 December 1979

Dear Ms Clutteur,

On behalf of Secretary-General Kurt
Waldheim, I would like to acknowledge your
letter to him dated 29 November.

The enclosures to your letter as well
as your record have been noted and he wishes
to thank you for sending them.

Sincerely yours,

Martha Aasen, Chief
Public Inquiries Unit
Department of Public Information

Ms Arletta M. Clutteur
Route 1, Box 152
Broadway, Virginia 22815

FAITH FULL

The President
of the Arab Republic of Egypt

الرئيس

Cairo,August   ,1979

Dear Mrs. Arletta M. Clutteur :

      Your letter and the very melodeous disk
of Labor Of Love " Poems & Songs " have been
received with great appreciation on August 27,1979 .

      This is why my answer is a bit late .

      First of all I would like to thank
you for taking the trouble of writting and sending
such beautiful " Peace Songs " .

      I seize this opportunity to express my
heart felt wishes of happiness and .good luck to
you and to all the people of your friendly
country .

                  Sincerely,

                  (Anwar El-Sadat)

Mrs. Arletta M. Clutteur ,
Broadway , Virginia 22815
Route , Box 152

2438 RAYBURN HOUSE OFFICE BUILDING
WASHINGTON, DC 20515-4606
(202) 225-5431
FAX (202) 225-9681
Sixth District, Virginia
www.house.gov/goodlatte

DEPUTY MAJORITY WHIP

REPUBLICAN POLICY COMMITTEE

CHAIRMAN, HOUSE REPUBLICAN
HIGH TECHNOLOGY WORKING GROUP

CO-CHAIR
CONGRESSIONAL INTERNET CAUCUS

COMMITTEE ON THE JUDICIARY

VICE-CHAIRMAN, SUBCOMMITTEE ON
COURTS, THE INTERNET, AND
INTELLECTUAL PROPERTY

SUBCOMMITTEE ON CRIME, TERRORISM,
AND HOMELAND SECURITY

SELECT COMMITTEE ON
HOMELAND SECURITY

SUBCOMMITTEE ON
INFRASTRUCTURE AND
BORDER SECURITY

SUBCOMMITTEE ON
CYBERSECURITY, SCIENCE, AND
RESEARCH & DEVELOPMENT

Congress of the United States
House of Representatives

March 18, 2005

Mrs. Arletta Clutteur
PO Box 1056
Broadway, Virginia 22815

Dear Mrs. Clutteur:

Thank you for sharing your inspiration for a flag symbolizing unity and world peace. I join a great many people in sharing your wish for world peace.

Over the years you have provided so much inspiration through sharing your faith with myself and leaders around the world. I also hope that one day, all nations can live in peace and prosperity. Individuals like you are the greatest step toward that vision. I wish you all the best in your continued work bringing your message and faith to leaders around the world.

Thank you again for thinking of me and if I can ever be of assistance to you, please do not hesitate to contact me.

With kind regards.

Very truly yours,

Bob Goodlatte
Member of Congress

RWG:ab

FAITH FULL

Jerusalem, June 20, 1979.

Ms. Arletta M. Clutteur
Route 1, Box 152
Broadway, Virginia 22815

Dear Ms. Clutteur,

I wish to thank you for the album you
kindly sent to the Prime Minister and to tell
you that the sentiments prompting your gesture
are very much appreciated.

With best wishes,

Sincerely yours,

Miss Yona Klimovitzky
Personal Assistant to the
Prime Minister

COMMONWEALTH of VIRGINIA

Department of
Mental Health and Mental Retardation

COEN C. PLASBERG
DIRECTOR

WESTERN STATE HC
BOX 2500
STAUNTON, VIRGINI
(703) 885-82C

June 16, 1980

Mrs. Arletta M. Clutteur
Route 1 - Box 152
Broadway, Virginia   22815

Dear Arletta:

Everyone I have talked with today has had the most marvelous things
to tell us about the lovely picnic at your home yesterday. Your love
of people certainly showed - staff said the patients had the best
time ever!

Opening your home and grounds for a picnic and festivities for the
patients was one of the most generous and thoughtful things you could
have ever done. I understand that there was more food than could be
imagined - and everything from the chicken and vats of barbecue, all
the vegetables and homemade rolls to the delicious desserts was simply
out of this world. You had to have worked all week to prepare and
organize this. We were so sorry that someone from our office could
not be with you all, but previous family commitments prevented this.

Many, many thanks to you and all of your family and friends who helped
make this Father's Day a particularly happy and memorable one for our
patients.

Sincerely,

(Mrs.) Jane Berry
Director
Volunteer Services

/jl

THE WHITE HOUSE
WASHINGTON

January 27, 1986

Dear Miss Clutten:

On behalf of President Reagan, I want to thank you for sending him an inspirational recorded message.

The President appreciates the spiritual sentiments which prompted you to take the time to remember him in such a special way. Messages such as yours help make his task easier.

With the President's best wishes,

Sincerely,

Anne Higgins
Special Assistant to the President
and Director of Correspondence

Miss Arietta M. Clutten
Route 1, Box 152
Broadway, VA 22815

Bennett's Recording Service

BENNETT'S RECORDING SERVICE
Live Recording & Duplication
130 E. Springbrook Rd. Broadway, VA 22815
(703) 896-2978

MAKING 8-TRACK TAPES A SPECIALTY
CUSTOM RECORDING SERVICE

WE, AT BENNETT'S RECORDING SERVICE WOULD LIKE TO
COMMENT ON THE "WORKS" OF WHITE DOVE.

THE FIRST TIME WE MET ARLETTA CLETTEUR THE
SCRIPTURE ,HEBREWS 13:2 CAME TO MIND,"BE NOT
FORGETFUL TO ENTERTAIN STRANGERS:FOR THEREBY SOME
HAVE ENTERTAINED ANGELS UNAWARES".

SHE WAS SO SINCERE AND HAD A CERTAIN GLOW ABOUT HER
THAT ONE DID NOT NEED TO ASK WHAT SHE WAS ALL ABOUT
AND WHO WAS THE "MASTER WRITER" OF HER SONGS AND
POEMS.

WE APPRECIATED THE OPPORTUNITY OF DOING THIS ALBUM
AND THOUGH ARLETTA DID HER OWN PRODUCING, WE FEEL
SHE IS TO BE COMMENDED.

FEW PEOPLE BELIEVED IN WHAT SHE HAD SET OUT TO DO,
BUT WITH GOD'S HELP SHE ACCOMPLISHED WHAT SHE KNEW
GOD WANTED HER TO DO.

MAY GOD BLESS HER IN HER WORK THAT ALL WHO LISTEN
WILL UNDERSTAND THE HEART OF "WHITE DOVE".

Justine Bennett

THE WHITE HOUSE

WASHINGTON

September 28, 1978

Dear Ms. Clutteur:

On behalf of President Carter, I would
like to thank you for your encouraging
message concerning the Camp David summit
on the Middle East.

The President deeply appreciates your
expression of goodwill and support, and
has asked that I send you the enclosed
copy of remarks made at the conclusion
of the conference. He hopes that you will
continue to pray for the leaders and people
of the Middle East during the period of
negotiations that lies ahead.

With the President's best wishes,

Sincerely,

Landon Kite
Staff Assistant

Ms. Arletta M. Clutteur
Route 1, Box 152
Broadway, VA 22815

Enclosure

*Sara and I send you and your loved ones
warm greetings from Jerusalem.*

*May the New Year bring you happiness,
prosperity and good health.*

December 2019

Benjamin Netanyahu
Prime Minister of the State of Israel

**Prime Minister's Office
Jerusalem, Israel**

Ms. Arletta Clutteur
9914 Phillips Store Rd
Broadway, VA 22815
USA

Labor of Love, an Autobiography

I was born May 24, 1936 in the Central Shenandoah Valley of Virginia in a little hollow called Bennett's Run west of Bergton, Va. I write poetry and songs. I am a homemaker, mother and grandmother. I work part-time as a U.S.D.A. poultry inspector. I am very witty and entertain, going to nursing homes, Veteran hospitals, mental institutes; I visit my local hospital and take retarded children on outings. I am not a dancer but have received comments like "she moves with a gracefulness", "it looks like she is floating", etc. I am involved in many church activities. I reach out to serve others and I try to bring a ray of sunshine to the elderly and reach out a loving hand to the needy. I am a service to others whenever I may be needed in my community and beyond.

Although my inspiration and work began here in the Shenandoah, it does not stop here. I was inspired in 1974 to send messages to Heads of Government beginning with the former President Richard Nixon, and the late President Anwar Sadat of Egypt., etc. As a gift to our nation, and for Father's Day in June 1979, I designed a flag and sent it to former President Carter at the

White House in Washington D.C. This was sent symbolizing peace and love among all nations.

In April of 1979, i released an album titled <u>LABOR OF LOVE: POEMS AND SONGS BY WHITE DOVE</u>. I revised into poetry and songs much of the messages that were sent to leaders of many countries. An album was sent to the President of Egypt-Anwar Sadat, Prime Minister Begin of Jerusalem, Secretary Kurt Waldheim-United Nations, President Jimmy Carter and many other leaders including President Ronald Reagan.

This album has not been advertised or promoted, only through recognition by Heads of Government. It was given as a gift not as a political promotion, a true story and message in each. The poems and songs were messages of encouragement during the Camp David Peace Negotiation. Goodwill and warnings of hunger often using illustrations; In 1974, I visioned people lined up at a table waiting for food. My husband and I were at another table where food was plentiful. Through this experience, I was motivated to illustrate a message. In 1974, I began giving people corn and saying, "plant the seed, share it with others, it's going to be a lot of hungry people". I am just an instrument, blessed are the ears that hear, and the eyes that see. Signs of hunger were sent forth years before world hunger made headlines.

FAITH FULL

The World knows not the love of my heart and the labor of my hands. I'm just another person; a smile on someones face is joy in my heart. Perhaps the tie is now ready for me to continue to go forward to share my talent, bringing laughter and signs of love to others. My name will be recognized by the leaders and people of many nations.

I came from a broken home, I never knew my father but have a wonderful mother. In later years I learned from an older friend that at 13 months, I became very ill, the doctor had no hope for my recovery. Mother stayed by my cradle and prayed. She did not lose hope or faith. That night by 8:00 p.m. I was very ill, and by 8:00 a.m. the very next morning my mother saw that life was in me. She worked and struggled, picking up odd jobs, even scrubbing chicken-house floors to earn a few cents. Poor in material things yet very rich. She remarried and I learned what a real father was like. I have six half brothers and two half sisters. I remember the hard times, but they were the good times; if there was one piece of pie on the plate, a bit was shared and all was happy. My parents never received a welfare check, mother would say "we will manage".

A Memoir of Arletta Clutteur

I did not have the opportunity as other children had or have today and the excitement of receiving a high school diploma. I worked in homes babysitting. I did not use the money to forward my education, I used the money to buy my brothers new clothes. The knowledge I have is self-learning and the greatest teacher is the teacher of the Universe.

New Year's Eve in 1952, I met a wonderful Frenchman with a great sense of humor and it was love at first sight. On February 14, 1953, we were married The roots of his family include the Cherokee Indian. My husband gave me the title of "White Dove",. We share the same values of honesty, family ties, friendship, love and concern for others highly.

In 1962, I was hospitalized for cancer. Our three sons were very small. It was a hardship and struggle for us, but my husband was very brave and strong. We have a wonderful family.

I ask for nothing but give freely, and am grateful that I may share with others and never ask for anything in return. I am not a wealthy woman in material things, yet very rich. God has given me many gifts, the greatest of all is love. A gift of love, I know is true, a labor of love to share with you.

In Peace, Love & Beauty,

FAITH FULL

Arletta M. Clutteur

(WHITE DOVE)

Photo Credit: Brandy Somers Photography

Any inquiries about the stories within or obtaining a copy of her music can be made directly with Arletta via her publicly available postal address.

Acknowledgements

To her sisters, Eula and Geneta, who always came to help and always brought their senses of humor. They've fueled Arletta from the very beginning. Her sisters-in-laws Joyce, Sharon, Renee, Dorothy and Juanita (deceased) have joined right in the choir. Also to her brothers who have helped the mission, as well as who have supported the women who love to serve their community and their maker.

To her remaining sons, Dave and Charlie, for their constant care and support, and daughter-in-laws Diane, Lorraine, and Stephanie for lovingly joining the family and all its quirks. Thanks also for bringing animals and children and grandchildren around keeping Arletta young and vibrant. A special thanks to Lorraine, who was always a sounding board and who diligently helped with the books when White Dove Tours was buzzing.

To June Riddle, Judy Emswiller, Susan Blaine and all of her friends who came to help in whatever capacity they could. Their lights shone bright so Arletta's light could reach broadly.

To Norvel's children who adopted her as their own mother and looked out for her even after their father was gone.

To her niece-in-law Debbie Clutteur who helps with so much now that age requires more and more help.

To Bob Corso and the family at WHSV-TV3, for their continued support and friendship.

To Brandy Somers Photography for the photoshoot and making Grandma feel as beautiful as she is.

To Joey Harris, editorial guru and friend of Lyndsey, for keeping this project on track and focused on the things that matter.

To Whitney Romanoff, cover designer and creator of incredibly, soulful, beautiful things.

To everyone that has made a positive contribution to Arletta's life, to Lyndsey's life and making the difference for these ladies to try for something meaningful.

About the Author

Lyndsey Clutteur DePalma is the author of *Ready: What to Expect When Starting a Business* and is the mother of two soulful boys. She is proud to have such forces of nature in her lineage to pass onto her children and their children. Honoring her grandmother in a short memoir was something that she prioritized amidst a pandemic, division of our country from racial inequality and political unrest, and a mindful divorce that marked 2020 the most transformational year, second to becoming a mother for the first time.DePalma is grateful to have such a unique, spiritual and impactful grandmother who has influenced her own character. While not everyone can enjoy the privilege of writing a book to honor their ancestors, through this experience, she sincerely hopes we all just take a moment to learn something new each time they talk to their families. There's so much to behold, if we can claim the time.

Made in the USA
Middletown, DE
25 March 2021